A GUIDE TO PLAYING THE SCRABBLE® BRAND CROSSWORD GAME

Gyles Brandreth

A FIRESIDE BOOK
Published by Simon & Schuster, Inc.
New York

Copyright © 1981, 1985 by Gyles Brandreth

Board Design Copyright 1948 by Selchow & Righter Co., Rules of
Instruction Copyright 1948, 1949, 1953, and © 1976 by Selchow & Righter
Co., reprinted with permission.

A Fireside Book
Published by Simon & Schuster, Inc.
Simon & Schuster Building
Rockefeller Center
1230 Avenue of the Americas
New York, New York 10020

FIRESIDE and colophon are registered trademarks
of Simon & Schuster, Inc.
First published in Great Britain in 1981 by Sphere Books, Ltd.

Manufactured in the United States of America

Printed and bound by Fairfield Graphics

10 9 8 7 6 5 4 3 2 1

Library of Congress Cataloging in Publication Data

Brandreth, Gyles Daubeney, date.
   A guide to playing the Scrabble brand crossword game.

   Previously published as: The complete book of
Scrabble.
   "A Fireside book."
   1. Scrabble (Game) 2. Scrabble (Game)—Glossaries,
vocabularies, etc. I. Title.
GV1507.S3B73   1984   794.2   84-22122

ISBN: 0-671-50652-8

CONTENTS

FOREWORD

Over the years I have witnessed virtually thousands of Scrabble® brand crossword games, and I have observed and marveled at the skill of the very best and a few of the very worst Scrabble® players in the world.

In writing this book, I have attempted to create as complete a guide as possible and I hope it will prove of value both to the novice and to the aspiring champion. One feature that certainly makes it unique among books on the subject is that the word lists printed here are based on *The Official Scrabble® Players Dictionary*.

Let me say at once that there are no more civilized people on the planet than Scrabble® brand crossword players, but it can't be denied that passions *do* get aroused in competition. As the poet in this case, Robert Anderson, a devoted player, puts it so perfectly in his Ode to this splendid crossword game:

Where double beats treble but triple beats all
But you may have to settle for nothing at all
And chuck in your letters
And grope for their betters
And bring out a handful still worse than before;
Where your noun if deemed proper
Will bring you a cropper
And a cheat is worth more than playing fair
Where with just one E more
You've a staggering score
And your word may be rude—you don't care:
You are plotting and scheming, quixotically dreaming
Of clearing your tray and going out

But the next player's eyed
The place you had espied
And your staggering score's up the spout;
So you spring from your chair
Raise the board in the air
And smash it down hard round his ears—
Other players are crying
The letters are flying:
You're charged and end up with three years.
If your nerves are not icy, your temper is dicey,
When losing, you tear out your hair—
If you can't keep your cool
Then follow the rule—
When you dabble with Scrabble®, beware!

1
THE STORY

An Introduction to the History and Origins of the Game

The word game sold under the registered trademark Scrabble® was not invented overnight, nor was it invented by just one person. The game was developed over a fifteen-year period, from 1933 to 1947, primarily by two Americans, Alfred Butts and James (Jim) Brunot, but with considerable casual assistance from family and friends.

Alfred Butts was an architect by training. By 1931, because of the Great Depression, he was out of work. He had always had an interest in games, especially word-oriented games. As a boy, he was keen on anagrams, cards, crosswords, and cryptograms. By 1933, he had developed a vague idea for a game called Lexiko. Butts had looked at all the existing games and analyzed them. He found an abundance of dice games, card games, board games with men, board games with counters, bingo, and so on. Butts decided that what was needed was a game using words, and with his background and interests, he felt that Lexiko could be developed into a marketable game, from which he could expect to make some money.

In the earliest version of Lexiko, there were letters and racks, but there was no board. There wasn't even the concept of a point value for each letter. Butts had analyzed a large amount of newspaper text to determine the letter frequencies that he wanted for his 100 tiles. At this early stage, the idea of the game was to try to make a seven-letter word with the letters in one's rack. If a word couldn't be made, unwanted letters were returned to the pool of unused ones, and some replacement letters were taken. The first player to make a seven-letter word was the winner of that hand. Very simple, very straightforward.

The next stage in the development of Lexiko was the introduction of point values for the letters. Once a player had gone out with a seven-letter word, the other players were given the opportunity to play words of four, five, or six letters. Scores were calculated for the words played, and, in this way, a ranking could be obtained for the players. Butts' friends liked the game, so he decided to send it to various games manufacturers. None were interested. All of them returned his game, and none had any suggestions for improvements. Back to the drawing-board!

The next step in the game's development was the introduction of the board. Butts devised a board, introduced the idea of premium squares, and the concept that words should be played in an interlocking fashion, like a crossword. The game now had its name changed. It was called, simply, It. Butts resubmitted the game to the major games manufacturers, but it was again rejected by all of them. Their reasons for rejection were that it was too serious, too complicated, too highbrow, too slow, not pictorially interesting, and not glamorous enough. Interestingly, at this stage, the game was also rejected by Selchow and Righter, the company that eventually produced and marketed crossword and sentence games in the USA under the Scrabble® brand.

Butts' development of the game continued from 1933 to 1938, but every attempt to get it marketed led to rejection. In 1939, Butts was introduced to James (Jim) Brunot by a woman named Neva Deardorff. Brunot was a high-powered Government social work administrator, and Deardorff was a social worker. Deardorff already knew of Butts' game, and was something of a fanatic. She felt that Brunot might be interested in developing the game further and marketing it.

Anyway, Butts introduced Brunot to his game, which by this time was called Criss-Crosswords. With the intervention of World War II, little effort was expended in trying to market the game. One abortive attempt was made in 1942 by a man named Chester Ives. Butts made up the game sets himself, and Ives was to market them from his bookshop in Danbury, Connecticut. For various reasons, Ives took over the manufacture of the boards, but ran into problems. The exercise was fairly quickly abandoned, and so one more attempt to get the game off the ground came to nothing.

During and after the War, Brunot had been continuing to amuse himself with the Criss-Crosswords game. At Deardorff's urging, Brunot and his business partner, Lester Twitchell, contacted Butts again, still wishing to produce and market the game. This was in 1946 or 1947. Various discussions took place, and the outcome was that the game was resurrected, renamed, and plans made for launching the game. Logo-Loco was one brand that was almost chosen, but Scrabble® was the final choice. The game product was eventually launched in 1949 by Brunot through his Production and Marketing Company, in Connecticut.

In the first year of production, 1949, a total of 2,250 sets were sold, and the company lost money. The following year, 1950, saw 4,800 sets sold, but still the company took a loss. The third full year of production, 1951, saw 8,500 sets sold, but still the game failed to make any money for the company. Sales in the first half of 1952 were sluggish, and the prospects for the remainder of the year were not bright. But then, in the summer of 1952, the game took off with incredible success. Demand for the game was amazing. By 1954, Brunot's company had manufactured and sold 4½ million sets of Scrabble®. In the USA, it had developed into a veritable craze. All the major magazines (*Look, Life,* and *Reader's Digest*) were running pieces about it, and cartoons were appearing in newspapers and magazines.

What happened in the summer of 1952 that caused the game to take off the way that it did? New York City has a very large department store called Macy's. The chairman of Macy's board, Jack Strauss, had played the game in the summer of 1952 while on vacation with some friends. On returning to New York City, Strauss was amazed to find that Macy's did not stock the game. This led to a big order from Macy's, and they put a lot of effort into promoting it. It took off from there.

Soon after its boom period started in 1952, Brunot's Production and Marketing Company came to an agreement with Selchow and Righter about the manufacture and marketing of Scrabble® products. The arrangement was that Brunot's company would retain the rights to manufacture and market anything but the standard Scrabble® brand product. Selchow and Righter would handle the standard set, and the Production and Marketing Company would still be able to make deluxe sets, foreign language sets, and so on.

During this time, other word games were produced by Production and Marketing Company and Selchow & Righter Company which bore the Scrabble® trademark, such as Scrabble® brand RSVP and Scrabble® brand crossword game for juniors.

In 1971, Brunot sold outright all trademarks, copyrights, and claims in the USA and Canada to Selchow and Righter, with payments to be made over five years, finishing in 1976.

That, briefly, is the story of Scrabble's® development. Alfred Butts was the originator of the game, Jim Brunot provided the moving force in producing and marketing it, and Jack Strauss, the chairman of Macy's, was the catalyst who helped the game become popular. Neva Deardorff brought Butts and Brunot together.

2
THE SCRABBLE® BRAND CROSSWORD GAME

The rules of the game and how you play it. The rules interpreted and explained. The different regulations that apply in tournament Scrabble®.

THE EQUIPMENT

The basic equipment in any set of Scrabble® consists of a board, 100 letter tiles, four racks, and a bag. The bag is for keeping the letter tiles in when a game is not in progress, and is also for keeping unused letter tiles in while a game is in progress. The racks are for players to keep their letter tiles on during the course of a game. The board measures 15 squares by 15 squares, and squares are of five different types, colored tan, light blue, dark blue, pink, and red. The gray squares are the "nonpremium" squares, and the other colored ones are the "premium" squares. Precisely how the different squares are to be used during the game is explained later.

The numbers of the different types of squares are as follows:

164 tan squares
24 light blue squares
12 dark blue squares
17 pink squares
 8 red squares

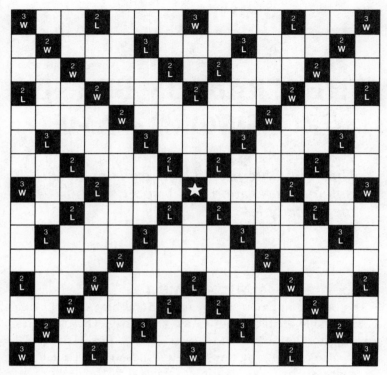

FIGURE 1

The light blue squares are called the double-letter-score squares; the dark blue squares are called the triple-letter-score squares; the pink squares are called the double-word-score squares; and the red squares are called the triple-word-score squares. *Figure 1* shows the layout of the squares on a standard board. The double-letter-score squares are marked 2L; the triple-letter-score squares are marked 3L; the double-word-score squares are marked 2W; and the triple-word-score squares are marked 3W. The board's center square, marked in *Figure 1* with a white star, is also a double-word-score square. It is distinctively marked

because the rules of the game stipulate that the first word
played on the board must cover this square. The 100 letter
tiles are made up of two blank tiles and 98 tiles bearing
letters and associated point values. The number of different
letters and their corresponding point values are as follows:

Letter	Number in a set	Point Value
A	9	1
B	2	3
C	2	3
D	4	2
E	12	1
F	2	4
G	3	2
H	2	4
I	9	1
J	1	8
K	1	5
L	4	1
M	2	3
N	6	1
O	8	1
P	2	3
Q	1	10
R	6	1
S	4	1
T	6	1
U	4	1
V	2	4
W	2	4
X	1	8
Y	2	4
Z	1	10
Blank	2	0

VARIATIONS IN EQUIPMENT

Deluxe versions of the board are available. Some of these have ridges on all four sides of each square on the board. These stop letter tiles from slipping about on the board as it is moved. To further ease the movement of the board, it sits on a raised turntable. The board can be revolved or turned without hitting the tiles in the racks.

Travel versions of the game also exist. The travel set is a miniature version of the deluxe edition and it folds in half for easy travel and storage. The tiles are made of hard wood also and remain on the board because it has ridges on all four sides of each square and these stop the letter tiles from slipping around.

OUTLINE OF THE GAME

The Scrabble® brand crossword game can be played by two, three, or four players. Played seriously, it is essentially a game for two players. The game consists of players forming interlocking words on the board, using the letter tiles. All words are to be connected, as in an ordinary crossword puzzle. Players score points for the words that they make. Scores are calculated depending on the point values of the tiles played and also the types of squares on the board that the letters have been placed on. Play passes from player to player until all of the tiles are exhausted, and one player has no more tiles left on his rack. The winner is the player who has scored the highest total number of points during the course of the game. The remainder of this book describes the rules governing where and how words can be placed on the board, how to calculate scores, and how to get the highest scores possible.

RULES FOR PLAYING

To begin with, all the tiles should be placed in the bag provided with the game and they should be given a thorough shaking. Alternatively, the tiles may be placed face down in the upturned lid of the box which the game came in, and then they should be thoroughly shuffled. From now on, the tiles in the bag or the lid will be referred to as "the pool of unused letters" or just "the pool." Each player now chooses one tile from the pool. The player with the letter nearest to the beginning of the alphabet has the first move. If two or more players choose the same letter and no other player has a letter nearer to the beginning of the alphabet, the players should return their letters to the pool and draw replacement letters. Once the first player has been chosen, the subsequent order of play is clockwise around the board. However, if players want to choose some alternative method for selecting the first player and the subsequent order of play, they may do so, but all players must agree about the method beforehand.

Once the order of play has been determined, all letters are returned to the pool and are well mixed. The first player then chooses seven tiles without looking at them, and places them on his rack. Other players then select seven letters in turn, each making sure that the other players cannot see his letters.

THE FIRST PLAY

Whichever player was chosen to go first uses two or more of his letters to form a word on the board. The word may be placed horizontally or vertically, so that one of its letters covers the center square on the board. Words may never be played diagonally. A player completes his turn by counting his score and announcing it to the other players. Scoring is described in detail later. The player's score is recorded by one of the players who has been chosen to keep score at the beginning of the game. After announcing his score, the first player then takes as many tiles from the pool of unused letters as he has just played on the board, ending up with seven tiles on his rack again. *Figures 2* and *3* show possible boards after the first move in each of two games.

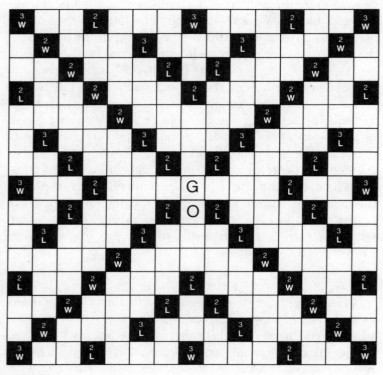

FIGURE 2

FIGURE 3

FIGURE 4

THE SUBSEQUENT PLAYS

After the very first move, players, in turn, add one or more tiles to those already on the board, forming one or more new words at each turn. Tiles may only be placed horizontally or vertically adjacent to a tile already on the board or one just played on the board. If the letters played touch other letters in neighboring rows or columns, they must also form complete words. Each player gets full credit not only for the new words he puts down, but also for modifying words that may already have been on the board. The score for a turn is the sum of the scores for each of the

FIGURE 5

words made, or modified, by the player at his turn. Words can be formed in three different ways, all or any of which could be put into effect at one particular turn. The three ways are described here.

1. A word can be formed by adding one or more letters to a word that is already on the board, turning it into a new different word. Examples are shown in *Figures 4–8*. In each, the word GO was already on the board. In *Figure 4*, the single letter T has been added to the end of GO, forming the new word GOT. In *Figure 5*, the single letter E has been

FIGURE 6

added at the beginning of GO, forming the new word EGO. In *Figure 6*, three letters, ING, have been added to the end of GO, to form the new word GOING. In *Figure 7*, two letters, SA, have been added at the beginning of GO, to form the new word SAGO. And in *Figure 8*, letters have been added to the beginning and end of GO, forming the new word AGONY.

FIGURE 7

FIGURE 8

FIGURE 9

2. A word can be formed by playing a word perpendicularly to a word already on the board. The new word must either use one of the letters of the word already on the board, or must add a letter to the word already on the board, making a second new word in the process. Examples are shown in *Figures 9* and *10*. In *Figure 9*, the word GO was already on the board. Four letters, WH and LE, are added to the O of GO, forming the new word WHOLE. As WHOLE is the only new word made, it is the only word for which points can be scored. In *Figure 10*, the word GO was already

FIGURE 10

on the board. The vertical word EATEN is now placed on the board, turning GO into GOT at the same time. Two new words have been formed, EATEN and GOT, and points are to be scored for both. The total score for the move is the sum of the scores for each of the individual new words formed.

3. A word can be played parallel to a word already on the board, so that adjoining letters form new words. *Figure 11* gives an example of this. The word LINED was already on the board. The new word HOMING is then played parallel to it, forming the new words HI, ON, ME, and ID at the same

FIGURE 11

time. All five of these new words score points. The total
score for the move is the sum of the points scored by each
of the words separately.

In all cases, after the first word has been played, across
the center square of the board, all other words played must
interlock with other words already on the board. No word or
words can be in isolation from the other words on the
board.

As well as forming words in the three ways described
above, it is possible to form words that are essentially

27

FIGURE 12

different combinations of the three methods. Examples are given in *Figures 12–14*. In *Figure 12*, the words GO, RING, WRITE, and TO are already on the board. The letters TTER are added to the end of TO, forming TOTTER, and also turning GO into GOT at the same time. In *Figure 13*, the words ATONE, AM, ME, GATE, SIN, and STOP are already on

FIGURE 13

the board. Using the A of GATE and the I of SIN, the horizontal word RATION is formed. At the same time, the vertical words RAM, TO, TOE, and ON are also formed. In *Figure 14*, the words GOAT and RAG are already on the board. The horizontal word MENTOR is played, turning RAG into RAGE, and forming the new words ON, AT, and TO.

FIGURE 14

EXCHANGING TILES

At his turn, a player may decide not to place any tiles on the board, or, indeed, may be totally unable to place any tiles at all on the board. In this case, any or all of the tiles on his rack may be exchanged for an equivalent number of tiles from the pool of unused letters. The unwanted tiles must first be removed from his rack, new ones are selected from the pool, the unwanted ones returned to the pool, and the pool then thoroughly mixed. A player must decide which tiles he wants to get rid of before taking new ones from the pool. A player cannot change tiles and place tiles on the board at the same time. He can do one or the other, but not both. Toward the end of the game when there are only a few tiles left in the pool of unused ones, a player cannot exchange more tiles than there actually are in the pool. If the pool has only four tiles in it, and a player wants to exchange five tiles, he cannot. He can exchange up to four tiles only, or decide to actually place some tiles on the board instead.

If a player wants to exchange his tiles on the very first move of the game, he is entitled to do so. The second player, who then becomes the first player to actually place a word on the board, must observe the same requirements as he would if he was the first player. Namely, he must play at least two tiles, and the word must cover the center square of the board.

The official rules do not impose any limit on the number of exchanges that a player may make during the course of a game. However, some players do impose such a rule. In any game where there is such a limit, it must be clear to all players exactly how many exchanges will be allowed.

The reasons why a player might prefer to exchange some or all of his tiles will be looked at in more detail later.

MISSING A TURN

A player is not allowed to miss a turn, unless he cannot make a word and there are no tiles remaining in the pool. He *must* either place one or more tiles on the board or exchange one or more tiles. However, some players are not particularly fussy about enforcing this rule, allowing players to pass as they wish. As will be seen later, there is usually little point in just passing.

BLANK TILES

The two blank tiles in the set of 100 tiles have no point value. They are each worth nothing. And yet, they are the most valuable tiles in the whole set. Just why this is so will become apparent later. A blank tile may be used to represent any letter that its player wishes. When a player puts a word on the board using a blank, he must state what letter the blank represents. Thereafter, the blank continues to represent that letter until the end of the game. The letter represented by a blank cannot be changed part way through a game. In the standard version, once a blank has been played on the board, it cannot be removed from the board. (There is a variant version of the game that allows blanks to be removed from the board, as long as they are replaced by the letters that they represent. The blanks may then be used to represent other letters when they are subsequently played.)

SCORING

A list of the point values of the different letters was given earlier. In general, the commoner letters are worth 1 or 2 points, the uncommon letters are worth 8 to 10 points, and the other letters fall between these extremes, being worth 3 to 5 points. The premium (colored) squares and the nonpremium (tan) squares have already been described. Now is the time to see how the point values and squares are used in calculating the score for a move made by a player. The five different types of squares (tan, light blue, dark blue, pink, and red) all affect the scores of the words played on the squares. The effects of the differently colored squares are as follows:

1. If a letter of a word is placed on a tan square, the letter scores the point value shown on the face of the tile. (In the figures in this book, tan squares are shown as white squares.)

2. If a letter of a word is placed on a (light blue) double-letter-score square, the letter scores *twice* the point value shown on the face of the tile.

3. If a letter of a word is placed on a (dark blue) triple-letter-score square, the letter scores *three times* the point value shown on the face of the tile.

4. If a letter of a word is placed on a (pink) double-word-score square, the letter scores only the point value shown on the face of the tile, but *doubles* the total point value of the whole word. That is, all the individual letter point scores are doubled. This doubling takes effect only after the effects of the double-letter-score and triple-letter-score squares have been taken into consideration.

5. If a letter of a word is placed on a (red) triple-word-score square, the letter scores only the point value shown on the face of the tile, but *triples* the total point value of the whole word. That is, all the individual letter point scores are tripled. This tripling takes effect only after the effects of the double-letter-score and triple-letter-score squares have been taken into consideration.

Once a tile has been placed on a premium square, that square has *no* premium value for any subsequent moves, even though the word in which the square is used may be modified. In other words, a premium square has an effect only for the first move in which it is used. Thereafter, it should just be treated as a tan (nonpremium) square.

Figures 15 and *16* give examples of how premium squares are to be used in calculating a word's score. In *Figure 15,* the word GO is put down as the very first word on the board. The G scores 2 points (its face value), and the O scores 1 point (its face value). The two letters together score 3 points,

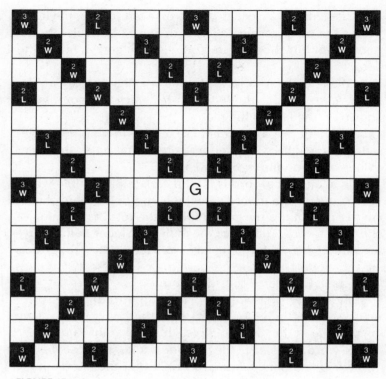

FIGURE 15

but, because the G falls on the star, a double-word-score square, the point value of the whole word is 3 points doubled, or 6 points. So the score for that particular move is 6 points. In *Figure 16*, the word WHITE is put down as the very first word on the board, the W falling on a double-letter-score square. The W is worth twice its face value because of this; that is, 8 points. The H, I, and T all fall on tan squares, and so score only their face value numbers of points (respectively, 4 points, 1 point, and 1 point). The E falls on a double-word-score square, and so has a value of

FIGURE 16

only 1 point, but causes the total point value of all the letters to be doubled. Thus:

$$W \quad H \quad I \quad T \quad E$$
$$8 + 4 + 1 + 1 + 1 = 15$$

But these 15 points have to be doubled, giving 30 points as the total score for the word. *Figure 17* illustrates another example. The word LIVE was already on the board. Using the L of LIVE, six letters were then played to form the word

FIGURE 17

CHILLED. None of the letters just played has covered a double-letter-score or triple-letter-score square. Accordingly, all the letters of CHILLED score points equal to their face values. Thus:

$$C \quad H \quad I \quad L \quad L \quad E \quad D$$
$$3 + 4 + 1 + 1 + 1 + 1 + 2 = 13$$

But because the word stretched across two double-word-score squares, the 13 points must be doubled twice; that is, quadrupled. So the word actually scores a total of 52 points. This should begin to demonstrate the power of the double-

FIGURE 18

word-score squares. *Figure 18* demonstrates yet another
example. The words EWE, ME, MAR, and TAR are already on
the board. Using the word TAR, the new word STARTLING is
formed. The second T falls on a double-letter-score square,
and so is worth 2 points. The other letters all score points
equal to their face values. Thus:

S   T   A   R   T   L   I   N   G
1 + 1 + 1 + 1 + 2 + 1 + 1 + 1 + 2 = 11

But as the word covers two double-word-score squares,
the 11 points must be doubled twice; that is, quadrupled. So

FIGURE 19

the total score for the word is 44 points. This should demonstrate the need to take into account the effects of double-letter-score (and triple-letter-score) squares before applying the effects of the double-word-score (and triple-word-score) squares. A further example is offered by *Figure 19*. The word EARN is already on the board. It is subsequently turned into YEARNINGS. The I falls on a double-letter-score square and the S falls on a triple-word-score square. The total score of the word is calculated thus:

$$
\begin{array}{ccccccccc}
Y & E & A & R & N & I & N & G & S \\
4 + & 1 + & 1 + & 1 + & 1 + & 2 + & 1 + & 2 + & 1 = 14
\end{array}
$$

But the 14 points must be tripled, because of the premium square covered by the S. So the total score for the word is 42 points.

So, to summarize: When a word is formed and it covers more than one premium square *at that move*, the total score for the word is calculated by working out the scores for all the letters individually, taking into account the effects of the double-letter-score and triple-letter-score squares, adding them together, and then doubling or tripling the score as necessary, depending on how many double-word-score and triple-word-score squares have also been covered *at that move*.

If a blank tile is placed on a double-letter-score or triple-letter-score square, it has no effect. Twice nothing is nothing, and three times nothing is nothing. But, if the blank tile falls on a double-word-score or triple-word-score square, the point value of the whole word is still doubled or tripled, as necessary, even though the blank itself contributes no points at all.

If two or more words are formed at the same turn, they are all scored, as described above, and the total score for the turn is the sum of the scores for all of the words made. Common letters are counted, with their full premium values, if any, in the score for each of the words in which they occur. *Figure 20* offers an example. The words NICE and AN are already on the board. The word ACHE is now played horizontally, turning AN into CAN at the same time. Because the C falls on a triple-letter-score square, it contributes 9 points to both ACHE and CAN. Thus:

$$
\begin{array}{ccccccccc}
A & & C & & H & & E & & \\
1 & + & 9 & + & 4 & + & 1 & = & 15
\end{array}
$$

and

$$
\begin{array}{ccccccc}
C & & A & & N & & \\
9 & + & 1 & + & 1 & = & 11
\end{array}
$$

FIGURE 20

The 15 points and the 11 points have to be added together to get the total score for the move. The total is, of course, 26 points.

A powerful example of the cumulative effect of premium squares is given in *Figure 21*. The words FRO, CHAR, HALF, OFTEN, ON, and ONE are already on the board. Playing the single letter Z just to the left of ONE causes two new words to be formed, ZONE and FROZE. Because the Z occurs in both words, it contributes its tripled score (because it is on a triple-letter-score square) to both words. Thus:

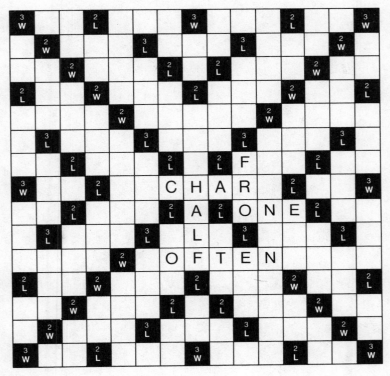

FIGURE 21

$$\begin{array}{ccccc} Z & O & N & E \\ 30 + & 1 + & 1 + & 1 & = 33 \end{array}$$

and

$$\begin{array}{ccccc} F & R & O & Z & E \\ 4 + & 1 + & 1 + & 30 + & 1 & = 37 \end{array}$$

The 33 points and the 37 points have to be added together to get the total score for the move. The total is, of course, 70 points. Just for playing one letter!

FIGURE 22

Once the basic method of scoring is mastered, even the most complicated of cases should offer no problems. Consider the example shown in *Figure 22*. The words HORN, MOON, MOUNT, TANGO, TAP, ON, and TIN are already on the board. By playing the letters SIGH in front of the T of TIN, and the letter G after TIN, the horizontal word SIGHTING and the vertical words TAPS and OH are formed. The total score is calculated by first working out the score for each word separately.

Thus:

$$\begin{array}{ccccccc} T & A & P & S \\ 1 & + & 1 & + & 3 & + & 1 & = & 6 \end{array}$$

But this has to be tripled as the S falls on a triple-word-score square. So, the total for TAPS is 18 points. The score for OH is worked out like this:

$$\begin{array}{ccc} O & H \\ 1 & + & 8 & = & 9 \end{array}$$

And SIGHTING:

$$\begin{array}{ccccccccccccccc} S & I & G & H & T & I & N & G \\ 1 & + & 1 & + & 2 & + & 8 & + & 1 & + & 1 & + & 1 & + & 2 & = & 17 \end{array}$$

But as the S and final G have both just been placed on triple-word-score squares, the 17 points have to be tripled, and tripled again, giving 153 points. The total score for the move is calculated by adding together the scores for the three words separately (18 points, 9 points, and 153 points), giving a total score of 180 points!

Another complicated example is shown in *Figure 23*. The words CODE, CAR, EAR, EDITOR, AID, OTTER, TEN, IT, RED, and ONE are all already on the board. The four letters C, H, N, and Z are added, as shown in *Figure 24*. This has resulted in the four words CHINTZ, HEAR, NIT, and ZONE being formed. You should be able to work out that CHINTZ scores 56 points, HEAR scores 15 points, NIT scores 3 points, and ZONE scores 26 points; giving a total score of exactly 100 points. Using a high-value letter in two words and doubling the score for each word, as the Z has done here, usually brings in a considerable score. So much the better, too, if you can incorporate a double-letter-score or triple-letter-score square with a high-value letter (like the H here).

FIGURE 23

THE 50-POINT BONUS

If a player uses all seven of his tiles at a single turn, not only does he get the score for that move, worked out as described above, but he also gets a bonus of 50 points as well. The 50-point bonus must be added after the effects of any premium squares have been taken into account. Obviously using up one's tiles in one go and getting a 50-point

FIGURE 24

bonus can boost a player's score quite dramatically, especially if this can be done several times in a game. The
importance of achieving such bonuses must be emphasized.
Later we'll discuss how to aim for such bonuses, working for
them rather than just waiting for them to happen by chance.
By chance, they happen very infrequently; by design, they
can be made to happen a good deal more often.

FIGURE 25

Figure 25 offers an example of a move that uses up all seven of a player's letters at one turn. The word REVOKES is played with the R falling on the center square and the K falling on the double-letter-score square. The score for the word is 19 points, doubled, plus the 50-point bonus, giving a total score of 88 points for the move. Note the importance of ensuring that the highest value letter falls on the double-

FIGURE 26

letter-score square. If REVOKES had been played as in *Figure 26*, with the V on the double-letter-score square on the opposite side of the board, then it would only have scored 86 points. If the player had placed the word so that any of the letters other than K or V fell on the double-letter-score square, as in *Figure 27*, the total score would have been only 80 points.

FIGURE 27

FIGURE 28

Even less desirable, the player might have played the word so that none of the letters fell on a double-letter-score square, as in *Figure 28*. This scores 78 points. Even when playing words that involve 50-point bonuses, you should not ignore chances to maximize the scores achieved from the letters in the words. The simple example offered here demonstrates a 10-point difference between the best and worst places for the word REVOKES played at the first turn of a game. The same principle should be borne in mind, of course, even when you are not playing for bonuses.

FIGURE 29

To ensure that you fully understand the scoring when 50-point bonuses are involved, *Figure 29* offers five examples of bonus words. The first player puts down the word ACTIONS. (The C is on a double-letter-score square and the whole word covers a double-word-score square.) The total score for this is 74 points. The second player follows this with SHUTTING, scoring 98 points. (This covers two double-word-score squares, but no double-letter-score or triple-letter-score squares.) The third word played is NEOPHYTE, using the N of ACTIONS. This scores 110 points. (Note that the H falls on a double-letter-score square and the word covers a triple-word-score square.) TOUCHILY is played as the fourth word. No premium squares at all are covered, so the word scores only 66 points. The fifth word played is DOUBTING, using the T of TOUCHILY. (The B falls on a double-letter-score square and the word covers two triple-word-score squares.) The total score for the word is 185 points! Of course, in real-life games, successions of 50-point bonuses do not happen particularly often. Even the most expert player would be pleased with three or four bonuses during the course of one game.

SCORING AT THE END OF THE GAME

A game comes to an end when *either* one player has used all of his tiles and there are none left in the pool *or* none of the players is able to make a move, and there are no tiles left in the pool. At the close of a game, each player's total score up to that stage is reduced by the point value of the un-played tiles left on his rack. If one of the players has used all of his tiles, his score is increased by the sum of the unplayed tiles on the racks of all of his opponents. Here is an example from a game involving four players. Suppose that just before the last move the scores of the four players were as follows:

player 1	155 points
player 2	195 points
player 3	215 points
player 4	170 points

Player 1 uses all the letters left on his rack, leaving none in the pool. Say he scores 10 points with his last move, bring-ing his score up to 165 points. Assume that his opponents are left with the letters shown:

player 2	AAEEO
player 3	QVX
player 4	M blank

The value of player 2's letter is 5 points, so his score goes down to 190 points; the value of player 3's letters is 22 points, so his score goes down to 193 points; and the value of player 4's letters is 3 points, so his score goes down to 167 points. (Notice that player 4 does not get penalized at all for being caught with a blank tile.) Player 1's total score is increased by 5 points (from player 2), by another 22 points (from player 3), and by another 3 points (from player 4), giving him 195 points altogether. The final position is this:

player 1   195 points
player 2   190 points
player 3   193 points
player 4   167 points

Notice how before he made his last move, player 1 was fourth. But by going out and catching his opponents for all their letters, he has leapfrogged over them all, and wins the game!

KEEPING TRACK OF THE SCORES

At the beginning of a game, one person should be chosen to record the scores. Precisely how this scorekeeper is to be chosen can be left to the players concerned. The scorekeeper should draw up a sheet headed with each player's name. Beneath each name should be two columns, one to record the points scored at each move, and the other to record that player's running total score. Suppose that players 1, 2, and 3 successively score 20, 15, 8, 65, 9, 25, 18, 30, 72, 8, 0, and 42 points (the score of 0 points indicating a change of tiles), the score sheet should then look something like this:

Player 1		Player 2		Player 3	
20	20	15	15	8	8
65	85	9	24	25	33
18	103	30	54	72	105
8	111	0	54	42	147

You should keep a running total as well as the individual move totals. This enables all the players to ensure that all of their scores have been recorded and to see how they are doing in relation to the other players at any stage of the game. Even if a player exchanges some of his tiles, keep track of this, too. In this way, all the columns should be of the same length at the end of each round, and it will be immediately apparent that someone's score has been omitted if the columns do not line up. Occasionally, players might want to reconstruct the exact course of a game. Having a record of the scores at every stage certainly helps this to be done.

WORDS

Up until now nothing has been said about the acceptability or otherwise of words that are played. What happens if a player spells a word incorrectly? Or if one player puts down a word that an opponent has not heard of? The official rules of the game state that any words found in a standard dictionary are permitted, with the exception of those beginning with a capital letter, those marked as being foreign, and those being spelled with an apostrophe or a hyphen. Abbreviations are not allowed, either. Because dictionaries can differ so much, it is wise for players to agree on a dictionary of authority at the start of a game. Some dictionaries contain only a few tens of thousands of words; others contain well over half a million. Dictionaries are published at different dates; today's neologisms may well not be in a dictionary published over a decade ago. Also, dictionaries have different attitudes to certain classes of words. For example, obsolete words are treated extensively in some dictionaries, and completely omitted from others; technical words get short shrift in certain dictionaries, but are treated much more fully in other dictionaries. So choose a dictionary that all players agree on before the game actually gets under way.

If a player is not sure about a word played by an opponent, the rules give him the right to challenge it. The word is then looked up in the agreed dictionary, preferably by both the players concerned. If the word is in the dictionary and does not break any of the official rules, the word is allowed, and remains on the board. If the word is not allowable, the letter tiles which have just been played should be removed from the board and returned to the rack of the player from which they came. This player loses his turn, and play passes to the next player. After a word has been played, the player should allow a reasonable amount of time to pass, to ensure that there are no challenges. If he selects some new tiles from the pool, and then the word he has just played is challenged and found unacceptable, there may be disputes about which tiles should be put back into the pool. Further, it saves having to alter the entries on the score sheet.

If the word challenged is unacceptable, the player takes back his tiles and loses his turn. If the word challenged is acceptable, the challenger loses his turn.

A word may only be challenged immediately after the turn at which it has been made and before the next turn. A challenge made after some intervening move is not allowed, even if the word challenged is obviously invalid. This is sensible as it saves problems about players returning tiles to the pool, picking up the tiles which have been played on the board in the interim, and adjusting the score sheet. Players should make sure that they are happy with all words played before the next move is made.

Most dictionaries include obsolete words, archaic words, dialect words, and slang words, though to different extents. The official rules do not bar any of these, but some players are unhappy about using such words, particularly obsolete ones. Again, there can be no objection to a "house rule" forbidding the use of certain categories of words, as long as all players understand and agree to the rule before play starts.

DICTIONARIES

Dictionaries have been mentioned in passing in the preceding section, but they will be looked at in a little more detail now. The rules allow for the use of any standard dictionary. Here are some dictionaries used by the Scrabble® brand crossword game players, with some relevant comments about each.

Webster's New Collegiate Dictionary (9th edition, 1983): This abridged dictionary has approximately 150,000 entries, a large number of which are proper names (clearly shown to have initial capital letters) and multiword phrases. Many words are shown with their American and British spellings. For example, COLOR and VALOR are both shown, with COLOUR and VALOUR listed as British variant spellings. It contains very few, if any, obsolete words, and contains many neologisms that have not found their way into other dictionaries.

There are also many other abridged or collegiate dictionaries that are widely used. The current five best-selling collegiate dictionaries are *Webster's New Collegiate Dictionary* (mentioned earlier), *Webster's New World Dictionary*, *The Random House Dictionary*, *The American Heritage Dictionary* (the New College Edition), and *Funk and Wagnall's Standard Desk Dictionary*. These college dictionaries are updated by their publishers far more frequently than their unabridged big brothers. Accordingly, they are much more likely to contain the latest neologisms, or new words.

Webster's Third New International Dictionary (1961): This unabridged dictionary contains about 450,000 words. No words at all are marked as foreign; because all can be found in English text, the dictionary makers have seen fit not to single out any as being foreign. It contains a large number of obsolete, dialect, and archaic words. It shows the plural form of every noun, all forms of every verb, and the comparative and superlative forms of adjectives where these are commonly found. This is something that no other dictionary does on such an extensive scale, and is one of the big pluses of this dictionary. As far as proper nouns are concerned, it lists them as all other words with a lower-case initial letter. Then, using a series of labels (such as "capitalized," "usually capitalized," "often capitalized," and "sometimes capitalized"), it offers some idea of whether the word is spelled with or without an initial capital letter. This can all be somewhat confusing for the Scrabble® player!

Among other unabridged dictionaries used by Scrabble® players, there's *The Random House Dictionary of the English Language*, published since 1966. It contains thousands of capitalized proper names scattered throughout.

The Official Scrabble® Players Dictionary: Probably the most practical dictionary for the American Scrabble® crossword game player is *The Official Scrabble® Players Dictionary*, published by G & C Merriam, the publishers of the authoritative Merriam-Webster dictionaries. This is the dictionary of first reference for all official Scrabble® Players® tournaments in the United States and Canada, and is widely used by many clubs across both countries. *The Official Scrabble® Players Dictionary* (OSPD) was edited solely with Scrabble® in mind. It is not intended to serve as a general dictionary of English, and many important features of general dictionaries have been omitted because they are largely irrelevant to the play of the game. Only words that are permissible in Scrabble® are included in the OSPD. Thus, proper names, hyphenated words, apostrophized words, foreign words, and abbreviations have been omitted. Several current desk dictionaries were used in compiling the OSPD. Words that exceed eight letters in length and are not inflected forms of words entered in the dictionary are not in the OSPD, and should be looked up in another dictionary like *Webster's New Collegiate Dictionary,* or a similar dictionary published by Random House or Funk and Wagnall. The OSPD shows the plural forms of all nouns, the derivative forms of all verbs, and the comparative and superlative forms of adjectives and adverbs where permissible. The OSPD gives only very brief definitions for the words entered. The OSPD removes those often open-ended arguments about the exact way to pluralize certain nouns, or whether the superlative form of a particular adjective is allowed. The OSPD has been defined as the authority for all words used in this book, unless otherwise stated. All word lists presented in this book are based solely on *The Official Scrabble® Players Dictionary.*

3
SECRETS
OF SUCCESS

How to become a Scrabble® brand crossword game champion; a complete guide to becoming a first-class Scrabble® player.

THE HIGH-VALUE LETTERS

The fifteen letters worth 4 or more points may be thought of as the "high-value" letters. The letters, their point values, and distributions are given here:

Letter	Number in a set	Point value
F	2	4
H	2	4
J	1	8
K	1	5
Q	1	10
V	2	4
W	2	4
X	1	8
Y	2	4
Z	1	10

To get the most from these letters, you should attempt to combine them with the premium score squares, effectively multiplying their face values. If you want to use a double-letter-score or triple-letter-score square, obviously the high-value letter must be placed on the premium square concerned. But for the double-word-score and triple-word-score squares, the high-value letter may occur anywhere in the word played, just so long as the word itself covers the premium square concerned. Much better even is to use a high-value letter on a double-letter-score or triple-letter-score square and also to make the whole word in which it appears cover a double-word-score or triple-word-score square. In this way, the face values of the high-value letters can be multiplied even more. Often there is little point in making a longer word unless it gives you a considerably higher score or it enables you to get rid of letters from your rack that you don't want. Elsewhere in this book is a complete list of all the three-letter words from *The Official Scrabble® Players Dictionary*. There are also lists of words that have four or five letters and which have one or more of the four highest value letters, JQXZ. Here is a small collection of four- and five-letter words that use at least two of the letters FHKVWY. You are bound to be able to think of others to add to these lists.

ASHY	FURY	NAVY	WAIF
AVOW	HALF	OFAY	WALK
AWRY	HATH	OKEH	WAVY
AYAH	HEWN	PHEW	WHIT
ENVY	HIVE	RIFF	WIVE
EYRY	HOVE	SHAW	WYCH
FAKE	HOWL	SHIV	YAFF
FIEF	KAPH	SWAY	YAWN
FIVE	KERF	THEW	YERK
FLAW	KITH	TOWY	YEUK
FLAY	KIWI	VERY	YOKE
FOWL	KNEW	VIEW	
FROW	LAKY	VINY	

ASKEW	FATLY	KOTOW	ROOKY
AWAKE	FERNY	KYTHE	ROWTH
AWASH	FEVER	LARKY	SHAKY
AWFUL	FLYER	LAWNY	SWANK
ENVOY	FUNKY	LEAFY	THEWY
ETHYL	HOOEY	NEWLY	VEERY
EVERY	HOWFF	NIFTY	VIEWY
EVOKE	HUFFY	OFFAL	VINYL
FAERY	HULKY	RAWLY	VROUW
FAITH	IVORY	RAYAH	WAVEY
FAKER	KEEVE	REIFY	

If you find yourself with several high-value letters and there is no way that you can use any on a premium square, what should you do? The best bet is to use the letters as quickly as possible, scoring as many points as you can. If you can't use any premium square, so be it. Some players would suggest that you hold on to the high-value letters hoping that an opportunity to use a premium square will arise in the next few turns. Generally, this is misguided, though occasionally there may be exceptions. Players who advocate this approach tend to believe that high-value letters make high scores and the other letters make low scores. While this is probably true for novices, it just is not true for advanced players. The advanced player will usually manage to use his lower-value letters for a much higher score ultimately. The advice given here is this: if you are holding high-value letters and there are no premium squares that you can use, get rid of the letters as soon as possible, hoping that you will pick up more useful letters for your next turn. This is particularly true for FJKQVXZ, which are not quite so versatile as HWY. After all, there is little point in waiting for three or four turns to get your Q on a triple-letter-score if in the meantime you have scored a mere handful of points on each of your turns.

Having offered this advice, though, you will find that there are occasionally genuine exceptions to it. Ultimately, you must assess whether it is worth playing a high-value letter now for less points than you might get if you played it later on. How many points are you likely to score while you are waiting? How long will you have to wait? Is your opponent likely to use the premium squares that you have your eye on anyway? And so on.

PREMIUM SQUARES

Playing Scrabble® well and scoring highly require that you always be aware of the relative values of different premium squares, the letters on your rack, and their possible combinations. Before putting down the first word that springs to mind, look for the alternatives. How many points would you get from each word? Though one may score more highly than another, it might use letters that you would rather hang on to for a while. If you want to make the lower-scoring move, by all means do so. Just be aware of all the options. Consider the example shown in *Figure 30*. The words LAME and IRE are already on the board, and you have the letters AEFKLRY on your rack. Your first thought might be to use the I of IRE and the letters FARY from your rack to make the word FAIRY. This has both the F and the Y covering triple-letter-score squares, and is worth a total of 27 points. With a little more thought you might have seen FLAKE and FIRE (with the F in front of IRE) for 31 points. Using the A of LAME and the letters FLKY from your rack, you could put down FLAKY for 31 points. Again, the F and Y both cover triple-letter-score squares. Having spotted FLAKY, you might consider repositioning it so that the F comes in front of IRE. This would cover a double-word-score square, and the total score is 37 points. If you spotted the double-letter-score square in front of LAME, you would have thought of FLAME and a possible five-letter word stretching down to the F or down from the F, so that it covered a double-word-score square. FLAKE and FLAME would be worth 46 points; but FLAKY and FLAME would be worth 52 points. Other possibilities that you ought to have seen, and rejected, are these:

FIGURE 30

using the L of LAME and FAKY from your rack, make FLAKY for 30 points; using the L of LAME and the letters ALKY from your rack, make the word ALKYL across either of the two double-word-score squares for 24 points. Finally, you should have considered using the I of IRE and all seven of your letters to make the word FREAKILY, with the A and the Y falling on the triple-letter-score squares. This would be worth a magnificent 78 points. (Don't forget that there is a 50-point bonus for using all seven of your letters at one turn.)

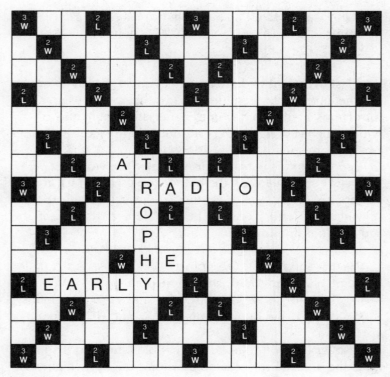

FIGURE 31

Figure 31 offers another example. The words AT, RADIO, TROPHY, HE, and EARLY are already on the board. On your rack are the letters DEHKOPY. Before putting down any letters at all, enumerate the possibilities. Here are some of them:

PIKE (18 points); POKY (21 points); HOOKED (24 points); POKED and EAT (31 points); YOKED and EAT (33 points); PEEKED (38 points); POKED and HEP (47 points); YOKED and HEY (51 points); POKED and DEARLY (54 points);

YOKED and DEARLY (57 points); YOKE and YEARLY (61 points); DOPEY and YEARLY (61 points); POKY and PEARLY (62 points).

The last five of these demonstrate that you should always be on the lookout for premium squares that can be used in two directions at the same time, especially when one of the words involved also covers a double-word-score or triple-word-score square.

Figure 32 offers yet another example. The words HE, HAT, and HOT are already on the board, and on your rack are the letters AESTWXY. Again, list the various possibilities before placing any letters on the board. Here are some of the possibilities in this case:

WAXES and SHOT (37 points); WAX, HA, and OX (43 points); WAXY, WHAT, and AE (46 points); WAX, WO, and EX (51 points); WAXES, HA, OX, and HATE (53 points); WAXY, WO, and EX (55 points); WAXY and HEX (62 points).

Be especially on the lookout for triple-letter-score squares like the one in this example when you have high-value letters. The score can really mount up when a high-value letter is tripled in two words.

WHAT TO DO WITH THE Q

Many Scrabble® players just don't know how to handle the Q. If you treat it right, you can get good scores from it; if you misuse it, you will find yourself in trouble. There are very few words in *The Official Scrabble® Players Dictionary* with Q not followed by a U. There are QAID, QINDAR, QINTAR, QIVIUT, QOPH, and FAQIR. BUQSHA is a Q word that could arouse a challenge while scoring well. Note the position of the U. You can assume that you will usually need a U or a blank to go with your Q. When you first pick up the Q, determine how many U's are already on the board and

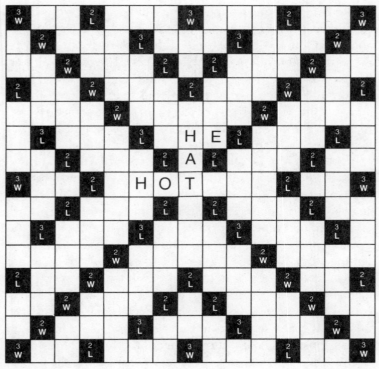

FIGURE 32

how many are left to come. If any of the U's on the board is in a position such that you can use it in conjunction with your Q, then do so immediately. Don't be too bothered that you have not managed to play your word on some premium square. Just be pleased that you have got rid of the Q without too many problems. If your word does manage to cover a premium square, well, so much the better.

Many players feel that the Q is a valuable letter to have because of its 10-point face value. These players dislike using the Q for anything less than big scores, and this is where they get into trouble. They will hold on to the Q for several turns until they manage to pick up a U or a blank, and then they will wait until a triple-letter-score square presents itself for them to put their Q on. They may well wait for six or seven turns, just to triple their Q. Meanwhile, their opponent is forging ahead! If, while holding on to the Q and waiting for a U to appear, a player can make some reasonable interim scores (say, 25 to 35 points for each turn), then this can be justified.

If you have the Q, all the U's have been played, and none can be used in conjunction with your Q, what do you do? Exchange the Q. Put it back in the pool of unused letters and select a replacement. This is the time to be ruthless. This will invariably be your best option, especially if the end of the game is near and there is a good chance of your opponent getting stuck with the Q. Even in situations where there are still U's to be played, you would be well advised to consider exchanging the Q, along with any other undesirable letters on your rack. Once you have put the Q back, there is the possibility that you will pick it up again. Even so, you should still seriously think about exchanging the horrid letter.

The OSPD has only one three-letter word using the Q. It is QUA. All the four- and five-letter words that have a Q and are in the OSPD are included in the list of words having the letters JQXZ, elsewhere in this book. Try to memorize some of them.

Of course, if you are fortunate enough to have a Q and a U together on your rack, you are urged to try to use them as soon as possible. As before, look carefully at the board, and enumerate the alternatives. Only when you are sure that you have found the best move should you actually start putting your letters on the board.

Figure 33 offers an example. The words TRAINER, REED, and ASTERN are already on the board, and your letters are ENQRSUY. Here are the options:

FIGURE 33

QUERY and REEDY (27 points); QUEST (28 points); QUA (32 points); QUAY (32 points); QUEER (36 points); QUERNS and REEDS (38 points); QUEAN (48 points); QUERY and EASTERN (81 points); QUEYS and TRAINERS (105 points).

If you don't know words like QUERN, QUEAN, and QUEY, look them up in the OSPD, find out what they mean, and then remember them. You are bound to need them.

THE MEDIUM-VALUE LETTERS

There are fifteen medium-value letters in a set, the same number as there are high-value letters. Their point values and distributions are given here:

Letter	Number in a set	Point value
B	2	3
C	2	3
D	4	2
G	3	2
M	2	3
P	2	3

The advice given earlier for the fifteen high-value letters applies to the medium-value letters, though to a lesser extent. The rewards of using the medium-value letters, whether they fall on premium squares or not, are usually not so great as for high-value letters. Many times there will be no great point in striving to make a play that just ends up with a G, say, on a double-letter-score square. However, do watch out for combinations of premium squares when you have medium-value letters. If you can double the point value of a letter and then double or even triple the score for the whole word, that can be well worth doing.

The medium-value letters cannot be considered in isolation, though. There will be many occasions when you have to use them in combination with the high-value letters and the low-value letters. Here are two lists of words, having four letters and five letters, that use low-value, medium-value, and high-value letters.

ABYE	BEVY	CHOW	DHAK
AHEM	BOGY	CHUM	DYNE
BABY	BOOK	DAWK	ECHO
BATH	CHEZ	DEWY	GYVE

68

HOMY	OBEY	RUCK	UPBY
KERB	OPAH	SHIM	WRAP
LACY	PALY	SKIP	YACK
LIMY	PHEW	SPEW	YAUP
MICK	POKY	TIDY	
MONK	PUNK	TYPE	

BARKY	CYDER	ITCHY	RETCH
BATIK	DEIFY	LIMEY	RUGBY
BENDY	DOGGY	MACAW	SPOOF
BHANG	DWARF	MATEY	THUMB
BITCH	EMBOW	MUCKY	VELDT
BLIMY	EPHOD	MUFTI	WHELM
BRAVO	GAWKY	NYMPH	WISPY
CACHE	GHYLL	OGIVE	YERBA
CHAMP	HOMEY	PIGMY	
CHINE	IMPLY	PYLON	

THE LOW-VALUE LETTERS

In addition to the fifteen high-value letters and the fifteen medium-value letters, there are seventy others, sixty-eight worth just one point, and two blanks. As 70 percent of the letters are worth one point or less, players cannot expect to pick up high-value and medium-value letters throughout the game. Neither should they expect to make the bulk of their final score from the high-value and medium-value letters. How then is the player meant to handle the seventy low-value letters? How are they to be played so as to get high scores from them? Simply by playing for the 50-point bonus.

PLAYING FOR THE BONUS

To get high scores, you need to score 50-point bonuses by putting down all seven of your letters several times during the game. An expert player will often manage two or three bonuses in a game, and even six or seven bonuses on the part of one player is not unknown! Very rarely do bonuses just fall into your lap. They have to be worked at.

Even if you manage to see a seven-letter word from the letters on your rack, there is no guarantee that there will be any position on the board where the word can be played. And even if you can see somewhere to get your word down, look for the alternatives. There may be better places for your word to go; better in the sense that you might score more points, or better in the sense that the board might become more "open." Before putting your letters on the board, calculate the scores that are available to you. Just because you can see where you can score 72 points, say, you cannot afford to ignore the possibility that a position exists that would score you 85 points.

Even though you may be unable to see a word on your rack, you might well be able to use a letter already on the board to make an eight-letter word. Many novice players concentrate on looking for seven-letter words on their racks, and only afterwards do they look for somewhere to play them. The accomplished player is considering both the letters on his rack and the layout of the board. He is thinking about the positions on the board where a seven-letter word could go, often before he has even spotted the word on his rack, and he is also pondering the letters on the board that could be combined with those on his rack. He looks for free, available letters, and then begins to think whether any will combine with his seven letters.

Figure 34 illustrates the point that various positions on the board have to be looked at. The words JUNTA, RAIN, ON, and ILL are already on the board, and you are holding AGINSTY on your rack. You will, of course, have managed to see the word STAYING. Now look for the various places where the word will go. Firstly, the G or T could go on the front of RAIN, making GRAIN or TRAIN. GRAIN and STAY-ING is worth 71 points; and TRAIN and STAYING is worth 74 points. But RAIN can also take an S or a Y at its end, making

FIGURE 34

RAINS or RAINY. You could play RAINS and STAYING for 77 points. Unfortunately, you cannot play RAINY and STAYING, the latter across two double-word-score squares, because you would also have to make the sequence OA, and that isn't a word. You could put the S of STAYING on the end of ILL, making ILLS. This gets STAYING across a double-word-score square, and is worth 76 points. This is a particularly unattractive move as it opens up for your opponent the two triple-word-score squares in the rightmost column of the board. If he managed to make an eight-letter word stretching across both these premium squares, that would be bad news for you. Another alternative is to put the Y of STAYING at the end of ILL, making ILLY. This is worth 79 points. (If ILLY is a new word to you, just add it to your growing repertoire of useful words.) Can 79 points be bettered? What letters are there on the board which you might be able to combine with your letters? There's the second L of ILL, the J of JUNTA, the U of JUNTA, possibly the N of JUNTA, and the R of RAIN. The J seems unlikely, but should not be dismissed out of hand. Dismiss it only when you are certain that you cannot use it. The U of JUNTA is a particularly attractive possibility. If there is an eight-letter word with the U in the fourth or fifth position, then two double-word-score squares would be covered. Similarly, if there was another word, apart from STAYING, with the S or the Y in the fifth position, so that ILLS or ILLY could be made, then this could be played across two double-word-score squares, too. A last possibility hinges on RAINS or RAINY. Is there a seven-letter word with an S or Y in the fourth position, and having its third letter combining with the O of ON to make a valid two-letter word? If so, it could be played across two double-word-score squares. Continued racking of brains throws up no words at all that satisfy any of these conditions. Accordingly, ILLY and STAYING are played for 79 points. Notice the way the expert player's mind is working here. He is not so concerned about the letters on his rack; he is identifying places on the board where words would go, and then seeing how his letters can be fitted into these positions.

Figure 35 illustrates the point about making eight-letter words, using a letter already on the board in combination with the letters on your rack. The words CABLING, ARGOT, FIDDLE, OF, TIRO, SO, SLOOP, PEN, PHANTOM, ENDING, TOIL, and GO are already on the board. On your rack are the letters AEINRST. You should have seen words such as NASTIER, RETAINS, and RETINAS from the outset. Once you have become familiar with the lists presented elsewhere in this book, you will know that RATINES, RETSINA, STAINER, and STEARIN are also words that can be made from the

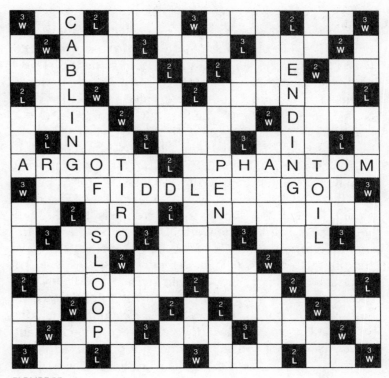

FIGURE 35

letters you have. The accomplished Scrabble® player will know all of these, and will dredge them from the back of his mind once he sees the AEINRST combination in his rack. The possibilities open to you are numerous. Here are just a few using seven-letter words:

RETAINS and TOILS (69 points); RETINAS and TOILS (69 points); NASTIER and RENDING (70 points); RETAINS and SENDING (70 points); RETINAS and SENDING (70 points); NASTIER, IN, and LA (74 points); NASTIER and TENDING (77 points); NASTIER and SLOOPS (83 points).

73

But what about eight-letter words? The possibilities are rife. Here are a few of them, and you may well be able to see others. The P of SLOOP could be used to make PAINTERS, PANTRIES, or PERTAINS, all for 64 points; or the same P could be used to make REPAINTS for a slightly better 74 points. The second O of SLOOP could be used to make NOTARIES, for 70 points. The R of ARGOT could be used to make RESTRAIN, for 70 points. The first N of ENDING could be used to make ENTRAINS, for 59 points. The second D of FIDDLE would help to make STRAINED, for 61 points. The B of CABLING would help to make BANISTER, for 62 points. The E of ENDING would help to make TRAINEES, for 70 points. The L of TOIL could contribute to ENTRAILS, worth 68 points: notice that the word PEN, already on the board, would be turned into PENT here. The C of CABLING could contribute to SCANTIER, stretching across a triple-word-score square and making 83 points. The M of PHANTOM could be incorporated into either MINARETS or RAIMENTS, both worth 83 points. The D of ENDING could be included in STRAINED, covering two double-word-score squares and scoring 86 points. An even better position exists on the board, if only you could think of a word to put down. If you could come up with an eight-letter word having M as its seventh letter, you could put the word down across the two triple-word-score squares in the rightmost column. That would score 149 points. So, don't just concentrate on the letters on your rack. Look at the board. See what letters are available, and work out whether they can be combined with the letters on your rack. This won't always work, but when it can, make sure that you don't miss the opportunity.

MAKING THE BONUS WORDS

Unless you actually work to achieve your 50-point bonuses, you are most unlikely to get them. Only very rarely will a bonus word appear by accident on your rack. How then should you go about getting bonuses? What do you have to do to make them happen?

The simplest way is to hold on to the easy-to-use letters, those worth one or two points, and the blanks, of course. Try to avoid having duplicates of letters, perhaps making an exception for E's and S's. Two of either of these letters won't cause you too many problems, but two N's or two U's may well be difficult to handle. Use up your duplicate letters as quickly as you can. Play them on the board in conjunction with the high-value letters that you are striving to get rid of; or return them to the pool of unused letters at the same time that you return your unwanted Q and two V's! For example, with the letters AAEENRT on your rack, you would be wise to play the duplicate A and E somewhere on the board. AE is an allowable two-letter word, so you should be able to dump the two letters quite easily. If you have to choose between vowels when deciding what to discard, ditch O's and U's in preference to A's, E's and I's. For examples, with AAIOOUU on your rack, if you can only get rid of two letters, use up the duplicate O and U, rather than A and O, or A and U. Better still, think about exchanging five or six of the tiles and getting some new ones from the pool. When getting rid of unwanted U's, consider where the Q might be first and how many U's are already on the board. You don't want to dump the last U only to pick up the Q!

When aiming for bonuses, you should try to have only two or three vowels on your rack, and get rid of those high-value letters as fast as you can because they restrict your opportunities for bonus scores. With a rack of letters such as AKNOOTT, you should try to play TOOK (or even KOTO, which is a word) somewhere, leaving you with ANT, a nice group of three letters.

Remember that the number of vowels (including Y's) is 44, and that the number of consonants is 54. In other words, there are more or less equal numbers of both. When you pick up new letters from the pool, you will tend to pick up an equal number of vowels and consonants. If you pick up an odd number of letters, the split will usually be as close to equal as is possible for the number concerned. Be prepared for vowels and consonants to come out of the central pool in roughly equal quantities. There's little point in playing RANT from a rack containing AAEINRT, leaving yourself with AEI, and then being surprised when you get two more vowels in your new letters. If possible, play the duplicate A only, and then you won't be too bothered whether a vowel or a consonant comes out of the pool when you take your new letter. Another example: given the letters AADEEII on your rack, you might decide to get rid of the duplicate letters, AEI. But to do this, you will probably have to use your only consonant, making the word IDEA somewhere on the board. This leaves you with AEI. Picking up four new tiles will, on most occasions, lead you to holding five vowels and two consonants. And you will still have your excess vowel problems! In this situation, you would be best advised to return your unwanted letters to the pool of unused ones and to pick some replacement letters. Either return AEI (leaving you with ADEI) or, probably fractionally better, return AAEI (leaving you with DEI). Returning AEI still leaves you with a 3-to-1 vowel–consonant split, and there could easily be two more vowels in the three letters you pick up; this would leave you with a 5 to 2 vowel–consonant split. The better move, putting back AAEI, leaves you with a fairly balanced rack, DEI. Why put back both A's rather than both E's or both I's? Because the sequence DEI seems potentially easier to handle than ADE or ADI. Given that you started with the letters AADEEII, it probably isn't a good idea to return five letters (AAEII) to the pool and pick five new ones. You must remember that the more new letters you select from the pool, the greater may be your chances of picking out an undesirable letter (another vowel, the Q, or one of the other high-value letters). Keep your letters balanced and under control. The randomness of the pool, induced by all the shaking and the mixing that it gets, will only serve to imbalance your hand. And you want to introduce into your hand as little random influence as possible. And you can do that by keeping down the number of letters that you exchange.

Never start off with the idea of making one specific word, even though you may have six of its seven letters. This is often the start of the road to failure, where, for three or four moves, you are hoping to pick up a solitary D, or a T, or even an E, and you struggle along making insignificant scores all the while that you are hoping.

The attraction of the one- and two-point letters is that they can be combined in so many ways with each other. The implication of this is that if you retain your letters in a sensible manner (concentrating on the low-value letters, avoiding duplicated letters, and keeping a reasonable balance between vowels and consonants), then you will fairly soon get the chance of playing all seven of your letters. Just look at these seven-letter words, all of them using one- and two-point letters. There are many more that you will undoubtedly be able to add to this short list. This little group should prove to you how easy it is to make seven-letter words from the letters worth one and two points.

ALIGNED	GANDERS	NEAREST	SEALING
ANGLERS	GRANITE	NESTING	STAINER
DARTING	IGNORED	ORATION	TOADIES
DEAREST	INSERTS	OUTSIDE	TRAINED
ERASING	LINGERS	READING	UNTRIED
ENTRIES	LOITERS	ROUSING	URINATE

Suppose that on your rack you have the letters AEIRSTY. You should play the Y. Put it down for the best score you can, but be prepared to accept five points if necessary. With your next pick-up, you are almost certain to get a letter that will combine with the AEIRST on your rack to make a seven-letter word. Watch out for these groups of six letters that combine well with other letters. For example, AEIRST combines with 18 other letters *(not* JKOQUXYZ), and these 18 other letters account for 80% of the tiles in a game. Elsewhere in this book you will find a list of all the words that can be made by adding a single letter to AEIRST. You will also find forty-nine similar lists, a total of fifty, for six-letter groups such as AEERST, AEINST, AENRST, EGINRT, and EINRST. Browse through the fifty lists. You don't have to learn all the words by heart, though many enthusiastic players do know most of the words. Get some idea of the six-letter groups that you should try to get on your rack, and learn as many of the words in the lists as you can. Then, when you have, say EENRST on your rack, and you pick up an X as your seventh letter, you won't be at loss for what to do. You will immediately recall the strange-looking word EXTERNS that is included in the lists. Of course, having found the word on your rack, you may run into one or two problems about putting it down on the board somewhere. As you become more familiar with the words in the fifty lists, you will realize that bonuses are not necessarily always achieved by using the one- and two-point letters. All the letters, medium-value and high-value, can be used in bonus words, as long as you have the right letters with which to combine them. Seasoned Scrabble® players are no longer surprised at the regularity with which a word like ANTIQUE (or even its anagram QUINATE) comes up. This is because the Q is in combination with easy-to-use, single-point letters. Much more surprising would be to see a word like QUICKLY played, having, as it does, a Q, C, K, and Y!

COMMON LETTER-GROUPS

When juggling with the letters on your rack, to see if you can make a word, it may help to bear in mind some of the groups of letters that frequently occur together. Here are fifty of the most common ones:

-ANCE	-ERY	-ION	-OUS
-ANT	-EST	-IOUS	OUT-
-ARY	EX-	-ISE	OVER-
-ATE	-GHT-	-ISM	PRE-
-ATOR	-IAL	-IST	PRO-
-CK-	-IAN	-IUM	RE-
DE-	-IC	-IUS	-TCH-
DIS-	-IED	-IZE	-TH-
-ED	-IER	-LY	-UM
EN-	-IES	-MAN	UN-
-ENCE	-IEST	-MEN	-URE
-ENT	-INE	-ORY	
-ER	-ING	-OUR	

BONUSES FROM BLANKS

Though the two blanks have no point values, they are the two most valuable tiles in the whole game. In a two-player game, it is generally unwise to play a blank score of less than 50 points during the first two-thirds of a game. If you follow the advice already given (about sticking to the one- and two-point letters, having no duplicated letters, and having a balanced vowel-consonant split), then, with a blank on your rack, you will usually be very close to getting a bonus. To use the blank tiles to score 30–40 points may well lose you 70–80 points a couple of moves later. Using the blanks to score 15–30 points, as quite a few novices do, is a waste, with the end-game situation being an exception. If the end of a game is in sight, you have a blank on your rack, and you suspect that your opponent is about to go out fairly quickly, you may have to use the blank for 10–12 points; for example, by using it as an S and pluralizing some noun already on the board. This is a pity, but there usually is not any alternative. Occasionally, though, a player will hold a blank right at the end of a game and manage to put down a seven-letter word. There aren't many games that are open enough at the end to allow a seven-letter word to go down.

FIGURE 36

HIGH SCORES FROM BLANKS

In the first two-thirds of a game, you should not hesitate to use a blank for a total of around 50 points, even though you may not get a 50-point bonus. That is, you may score about 50 points but not use up all seven of your tiles. *Figure 36* illustrates an example. The words ASPIC, CORAL, LAC, and AX are already on the board, and you have EHKRRT and a blank on your rack. You should turn LAC into LACK and make the word KART vertically, using the blank as an A, so that it covers the triple-word-score square in the board's bottom right-hand corner. This scores 51 points, and leaves you with HER. Using the blank as an I, you could have played HIKER and AXE. This would score 48 points, and leave you with RT. There isn't much to choose between these two moves, though the former is slightly better. Why? Because it leaves you with a high-value letter, the H. H is usually a fairly easy letter to use, and the other two letters, ER, aren't going to cause you any problems. If you had been left with something like FER or VER, then the 48 points move might have been the better one, even though it scores three points less.

One other consideration, concerning the Q and blank together. If you have a Q, a blank, but no U, what should you do? This is one situation where it might be worth using the blank as a U to score upwards of 30 points. If you cannot play the Q and blank for at least this sort of score, put the Q back in the pool and choose another letter. On most occasions, it is not wise to use the blank as a U just to get rid of the Q and score less than 30 points.

TWO-LETTER WORDS

The overwhelming importance of two-letter words and their proper use cannot be sufficiently emphasized. Many novice players who have not read the official Scrabble® rules carefully enough believe that two-letter words are not allowable. They are wrong. Nowhere do the official rules bar the use of two-letter words. Such words, as short as they are, are perfectly acceptable in Scrabble®, as long as they don't break any of the other rules. Two-letter words are important, usually not for the scores that they make themselves, but for the scores of the other words formed at the same time.

Consider the example shown in *Figure 37*. The words DOUBT, BOAT, THERE, EYE, and MEN are already on the board. Your turn is next, and on your rack you have EILMOPR. Are you able to make a word from these letters? And if so, where will you put it? You should be able to see

FIGURE 37

IMPLORE easily enough, but is there room to put it down on the board? There are two possibilities, both involving the use of two-letter words. Using the T of DOUBT, you could make IT vertically and IMPLORE horizontally, scoring 76 points. Or, even better, you could use the M of MEN to make ME vertically and IMPLORE horizontally. ME covers one double-word-score square, and IMPLORE covers two double-word-score squares. The total score here is a very healthy 102 points. Two-letter words are used frequently to add seven-letter words to the board in this way.

Some inexperienced players will only use such everyday two-letter words as AN, DO, HE, IT, SO, and WE. Experienced players will use any of the allowable two-letter words that are to be found in the dictionary that they are using. In *The Official Scrabble® Players Dictionary*, there are eighty-six two-letter words that are allowed. A full list is given elsewhere in this book. The list also includes their parts of speech (is it a noun? is it a verb? is it an interjection?) and their meanings. Some of the more esoteric words listed in the OSPD are given here:

AE	JO	OM	WO
DA	KA	OP	XU
ET	LI	PE	YA
FA	NA	UN	

Experienced players will be able to tell you immediately what these all mean, whether they can be pluralized or not, and so on.

The two-letter words that occur in different dictionaries vary to an astonishing degree. The number of words offered by a dictionary is generally in proportion to its size. So, the bigger the dictionary, the more two-letter words it is likely to contain. Given below are a few two-letter words not found in the OSPD but which can be found in other dictionaries not reviewed in the section on dictionaries.

DY is a type of sediment found in lakes
EA is a stream
FY is an interjection
HM is an interjection
IE is a pine
KI is a tree found in the Pacific
PO is a chamber-pot
YI is a term from Chinese philosophy
YU is a precious jade
ZO is a hybrid domestic cattle

FIGURE 38

To reiterate, none of these are in the OSPD, and none are allowed. They should give you some idea of the diversity which exists between different dictionaries, though.

The abundance of two-letter words also helps in getting rid of your unwanted letters faster than you otherwise might. Knowing that YA is an allowable two-letter word might help you in dumping an unwanted Y. There are other occasions when two-letter words can score very highly in their own right. Consider the example shown in *Figure 38*. On your rack are the letters BFHKMXZ, not a particularly desirable set! Your choices are many.

FIGURE 39

Using the A of PAL and the first A of ALWAYS, you could make MA and MA (20 points), or FA and FA (26 points), or HA and HA (26 points), or KA and KA (32 points); using the Y of DAYS and the Y of ALWAYS, you could make MY and MY (26 points); using the E of COMET and the O of MOB, you could make EH and OH (26 points), or EX and OX (50 points); and using the O of COD and the O of POD, you could make BO and BO (20 points), or HO and HO (26 points). Take the 50-point score. Continue picking off the triple-letter-score squares as long as you can.

Figure 39 illustrates the case of an eight-letter word being played and depending on several two-letter words. You have the letters ADEENRT on your rack. Those letters do not make a word. What to do? Play an E somewhere for a few points? Or exchange the E and get a replacement from the pool? Neither! Use the I of IS in the top row and make the eight-letter word RETAINED. At the same time, you will make RE, EX, TI, EM, DA and ATOLL. The net score is 176 points! But it could not have been done without those valuable two-letter words.

Figure 40 illustrates a similar situation, but not involving such a high score. The words INSERT, UNCLE, UP, JULEPS, HAT, and HE are already on the board, and on your rack are the letters GIINNOY. You would like to get rid of the duplicate I and N; and you would also like to use the Y. While YIN is a word, the best that you can score with it is 17 points, by making YE at the same time, using the E of UNCLE. Much better is to play YONI, underneath and parallel to JULEPS, making JO, UN and LI at the same time. This scores 36 points. Using the O for the extra 19 points is well worth it.

MODIFYING WORDS

Once a word is on the board, it can be modified by the addition of one or more letters in front of the word (prefixing), or after the word (suffixing), or by both together. Given here are some examples of modified words. The words on the left can be thought of as being already on the board, and those on the right are what they may be modified to give.

GO   GOT, GONE, GOING, GOLDEN, AGO, SAGO, TANGO, STINGO, AGOG, AGONY, EGOIST, EGO-TIST, ARGON, ZYGOTE, ONGOING, ARGONAUT, UNDERGONE

EAR   EARN, EARLY, EARTHY, EARNEST, BEAR, SPEAR, LINEAR, NUCLEAR, PEARLY, SHEARED, DREARILY, HEARTFELT

FIGURE 40

LINK   LINKS, LINKED, LINKING, LINKAGES, CLINK,
            SLINKY, UNLINKED, BLINKERED

EARTH   EARTHY, EARTHEN, EARTHING, EARTHLING,
            DEARTH, UNEARTHED, INEARTHING

PREFIXING WITH ONE LETTER

This is where just one letter is added to the beginning of a
word already on the board. It is very important, and for the
same reason that two-letter words are important. Namely, in
making a word perpendicular to the word that is being

87

FIGURE 41

prefixed. The new word formed by prefixing does not usually score that highly, but the word formed perpendicularly can, and usually does, score well.

Figure 41 illustrates this. The words BASH and WAKE are already on the board, and you have the letters AEILLST on your rack. After shuffling your letters for a while, you spot TALLIES. You cannot pluralize BASH by the addition of a single S. You cannot make WAKES and TALLIES because there isn't enough room to get TALLIES in. You have just two opportunities. Using the A of TALLIES, turn WAKE into AWAKE (for 75 points), or using the same A, turn BASH into

ABASH (for 77 points). The experienced player knows a large number of words that can be modified by the prefixing of a single letter. For instance, he will certainly know that DO can be modified to give ADO and UDO (a Japanese herb). He knows that the word OP can be modified by a single-letter prefix to give BOP, COP, FOP, HOP, KOP (a hill), LOP, MOP, POP, SOP, TOP, and WOP. Here are one hundred examples of words that can be modified by the addition of one letter. The added letter is shown in parentheses.

(A)BET	(E)MU	(L)OUR	(R)OLE
(A)BYE	(E)NOW	(M)END	(S)CAD
(A)EON	(E)PACT	(M)ETHYL	(S)HIM
(A)HA	(E)RADIATE	(N)ACRE	(S)ILEX
(A)HEM	(F)LAG	(N)EON	(S)LED
(A)IT	(F)ROW	(N)EVE	(T)ALAR
(A)NA	(G)LADY	(N)ILL	(T)ARE
(A)PART	(G)LEG	(N)OIL	(T)HEW
(A)TOP	(G)RIP	(N)ODDER	(T)IT
(B)AH	(H)AVER	(O)BIT	(T)OFT
(B)ILL	(H)EXARCHY	(O)GAM	(T)UMP
(C)ERE	(I)BIS	(O)GEE	(U)PEND
(C)ORE	(I)CON	(O)INK	(U)RATE
(D)ALE	(I)DEAL	(O)PAH	(U)REAL
(D)ILL	(I)LEA	(O)PINE	(U)SAGE
(D)RAFT	(I)MAGE	(O)RANG	(V)AGUE
(D)RIB	(I)ON	(O)VINE	(V)AIR
(E)DUCE	(I)ONIUM	(P)AEON	(W)ALE
(E)DUCT	(I)RATE	(P)EON	(W)RACK
(E)GAD	(I)SATIN	(Q)UIT	(X)EROTIC
(E)GO	(J)UNTO	(R)ACE	(Y)ARE
(E)LAND	(K)ART	(R)AFT	(Y)EAN
(E)LOIN	(L)AMP	(R)AND	(Z)ANY
(E)MIR	(L)AVER	(R)EAVE	(Z)INKY
(E)MOTE	(L)EAR	(R)ELATE	(Z)OOLOGY

You are bound to be able to think of plenty more to add to this list.

SUFFIXING WITH ONE LETTER

The object of suffixing with one letter is the same as that of prefixing with a single letter. Namely, to allow you to play a word perpendicularly to a word already on the board, modifying the word already on the board by adding a letter to its end. All the letters except Q can be used for suffixing. The experienced Scrabble® player knows a large number of these words. For example, he is well aware that BE can be suffixed to give BED, BEE, BEG, BEL (a measure of sound), BEN, BET, and BEY (a Turkish governor). Here are 100 examples of words that can be modified by the addition of one letter. The added letter is shown in parentheses.

COCO(A)	ANIL(E)	OBOL(I)	FAD(O)
EROTIC(A)	CAR(E)	SOLD(I)	FAR(O)
GAG(A)	FAD(E)	TAX(I)	HOB(O)
GAL(A)	HOP(E)	WAD(I)	HER(O)
LOT(A)	JAK(E)	YET(I)	OH(O)
MAN(A)	MAR(E)	HA(J)	QUART(O)
OCHRE(A)	TOP(E)	HAD(J)	TAR(O)
VILL(A)	ULNA(E)	DAW(K)	WIN(O)
VIOL(A)	YOW(E)	BEL(L)	CAR(P)
JAM(B)	SCAR(F)	EROTICA(L)	TAM(P)
LAM(B)	SHEA(F)	HOVE(L)	DEE(R)
MAGI(C)	KIN(G)	MIL(L)	LOVE(R)
MANIA(C)	RAISIN(G)	NOR(M)	TEA(R)
AMEN(D)	RAN(G)	WAR(M)	ULNA(R)
BAN(D)	BAT(H)	AIR(N)	VIOLATE(R)
LAR(D)	DOT(H)	CANTO(N)	WRITE(R)
WAR(D)	CAD(I)	FIR(N)	NEEDLES(S)
AGE(E)	IAMB(I)	PEE(N)	PAS(S)
AID(E)	MAG(I)	TEE(N)	PRINCES(S)
AMID(E)	MID(I)	ZOO(N)	WINDLES(S)

AIR(T)	SKI(T)	DE(V)	ALAR(Y)
AMEN(T)	EM(U)	RE(V)	FOG(Y)
CHAR(T)	LIE(U)	NO(W)	FIZ(Z)
ERS(T)	MEN(U)	VIE(W)	QUART(Z)
PUT(T)	TAB(U)	CODE(X)	SPIT(Z)

SETTING UP PLAYS

The reason for discussing single-letter prefixing and suffixing at such length is because the experienced Scrabble® player not only modifies the words that are already on the board, he puts them there in the first place, so that he can use them subsequently. Good players will often put down a word that they know is capable of being modified by a single letter at the beginning or end. There are two reasons for this. Firstly, it enables certain letters to be counted twice in the scoring process; and secondly, and far more importantly, it gives a potential place to put down a seven-letter word.

Consider the situation in *Figure 42*. The first player put down the word VYING. The second player, holding IL-NORTW, used the G of VYING and played GROW. This scored 8 points. He could have played GROWL or GROWN for 10 points, or even GLOW for 8 points. GROW is certainly the best move. He can use his L or N at a subsequent turn (the next turn?), making either GROWL or GROWN, and possibly get down a seven-letter word if he has one. GLOW would have been a pointless play, because the only letter that can be added to its end is S, and he doesn't have one of those. GROWL can only be suffixed with an S (making GROWLS) or a Y (making GROWLY), and he had neither an S nor a Y. GROWN cannot be suffixed at all. The first player follows GROW by playing MUGGY. At this stage, the second player is holding EGILNRT. With these letters he can make RINGLET and TINGLER. He now uses the opening that he has created for himself with the word GROW. He could play

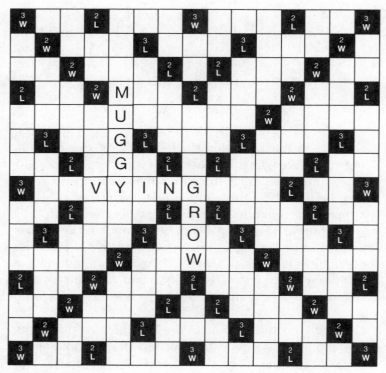

FIGURE 42

any of RINGLET and GROWL, RINGLET and GROWN, TINGLER and GROWL, and TINGLER and GROWN, all scoring 78 points. Had he not played GROW as his first move, he probably wouldn't have had a seven-letter word that went down on the board at his second turn.

When you set up plays like this, you always run the risk that your opponent will do something to wreck your plans. This is why it is much more difficult to get down bonus words in games with three or four players. With three players, you have twice as many opponents as you would have in a two-player game; and with four players, you have three times as many opponents. In three- and four-player games, setting up plays for yourself is considerably less important than it is in two-player games.

SETTING UP PLAYS IS A GAMBLE

When you set up plays for yourself, you are taking a gamble, the gamble that you are giving up the prospect of some immediate points for many more points a move or two later. What do you lose if it fails? What does your opponent gain if he uses your opening the way you had intended to do? Remember, he may be sitting there with a seven-letter word on his rack, just itching for an opening for it! Take into account your opponent's skill, the different letters that might be used, the chances of your opponent having these letters rather than the pool having them, whether you have opened up a valuable premium square, and, not at all a matter to be dismissed, your opponent's disposition. Some players will suspect that an opponent is setting up an opening and will block it at all costs. Other players, perhaps too generously, will not block such a set-up play, even though they know full well what you are doing. Other players, even more Machiavellian, will not block an opening for just a few points, as they want to use it themselves for a seven-letter word in the next turn or so. They are gambling that they can get down their bonus word before you can get down yours. Perhaps setting up plays is *not* a gamble, but more of a finely calculated risk!

EXCESSIVE CONSONANTS

The advice given earlier was to keep a balanced rack of letters—low-value letters, no duplicates, and two or three vowels. If you find yourself sitting on a cluster of consonants, though, even single-point ones, start getting rid of them. Exchange them and get some replacement letters from the pool, or play a word with several consonants in it. Here are fifty words that are top-heavy with consonants. You probably have your own favorites.

93

BRUNT	HATCH	OCHRY	THROB
CHALK	HITCH	PARCH	VELDT
CHAMP	HYMN	PECKY	VERB
CONCH	KETCH	PHEW	VETCH
CRWTH	KNELT	PHON	WHORL
DIGHT	LARCH	PSHAW	WITCH
DITCH	LYMPH	PSYCH	WOMB
DRUNK	MATCH	RHOMB	XYLOL
FILCH	MILK	RHUMB	YACHT
FIRTH	MYRRH	SHAFT	ZLOTY
GLYPH	MYTH	SYLPH	ZYMES
GNAW	NOTCH	THAW	
GRUFF	NYMPH	THICK	

EXCESSIVE VOWELS

If your rack contains an excess of vowels, either exchange them and get some replacements from the pool, or play a word with several vowels in it. Here are fifty words suffering from an excess of vowels.

ABOIDEAU	AUDIO	HOOEY	OLEO
ADIEU	AURA	IDEA	OLIO
AEON	AURAE	ILIA	OORIE
AERIE	AUREI	INIA	OUABAIN
AGEE	AUTO	IOTA	OURIE
AGUE	BEAU	LIEU	ROUE
AJEE	COOEE	MOUE	URAEI
AKEE	COOEY	OBEY	UREA
ALAE	EERIE	OBIA	UVEA
ALEE	EMEU	OBOE	ZOEA
ANOA	EPEE	OGEE	ZOEAE
AREA	ETUI	OHIA	
ARIA	EURO	OILY	

KEEPING TRACK OF THE TILES

In a two-player game, by the time that the last tile has been taken from the pool, you should know precisely what letters your opponent holds. Working out whether he has any high-value letters (FHJKQVWXYZ) is fairly easy. Working out which other letters he has is merely a question of counting up the letters on the board and your own rack, and then crediting your opponent with the missing ones. Once you know your opponent's letters, you should be able to work out what he is likely to do with them, and therefore how long you can prolong the game. For example, if he has the Q, all the U's are on the board and unusable, and both the blanks have gone, you have all the time in the world. Play out your letters one or two at a time, making the most points you can. You will invariably score better by playing them out slowly like this, rather than playing them out in just one or two longer words. Your opponent won't be able to go out with the Q stuck on his rack. Even if your opponent doesn't have the Q, it will still be useful to know that he has something like AAAIOVV. Again, his options are fairly limited, and he is unlikely to be able to go out for three or four turns. On the other hand, if you find your opponent holding something akin to AEILRST and there is a place to put a seven-letter word on the board, block it. If there is more than one place for the word to go, get rid of as many of your tiles as you can for as many points as you can.

Not only should you keep track of the unplayed tiles at the end of a game, you should try to keep a mental note of what's been played during the game. The high-value letters are fairly easy to mentally tick off as they are played, and the same is true of the medium-value letters once you have had a little practice. There is little point in hoping to pick up an M, say, if both are already on the board. Keep checking to see what's likely to be left in the pool during the later stages of the game. If seventy-five tiles have been played and the FFJKVVZ are still to appear, take care! You don't want to pick up all of them. In which case, try playing only a few letters at a time. You don't want to play six letters, select six new ones from the pool and find that you have picked up six high-value letters!

Also, keep track of the rate at which vowels and consonants are being played. Quite often, there is a flood of vowels in the early stages of the game, and this can lead both players into trouble later on when the consonants start to come out in unexpected numbers. The opposite problem occurs, too. A lot of consonants coming out too soon in the game, with relatively few vowels being played, can close up the board, making bonus plays difficult, if not impossible, later on.

END PLAY

Most games in which the final scores are within thirty points or so of each other are won or lost in the last few moves. Don't forget that when a player has used all of his tiles and the pool is exhausted, the scores of the other players are reduced by the sum of the point values of the tiles held by each player, and the score of the player who has gone out is increased by the sum of the point values of all the tiles held by his opponents. So, if a game is close towards the end, it is important that you try to go out before your opponents. Going out first in a game with three or four players is even more important than going out first in a game with just one other player. You are likely to pick up two or three times as many points from your opponents than you would in a two-player game. So, when you are near the end of a game, what can you do to improve your own score and to reduce your opponent's by as many points as possible?

First of all, try to get rid of your high-value and medium-value tiles. Don't get stuck with them if you can avoid it, or else your opponent will go out first and your score will suffer from the effects of the letters left on your rack. Either put those letters down on the board somewhere, or, if that isn't possible, put them back into the pool of unused letters and get some replacements. Suppose there are just three letters left in the pool and on your rack are AEFIQSV. Work out what the 10 outstanding tiles are (the seven on your opponent's rack plus the three in the pool), just to make sure that there are no nasty surprises in store for you (like two Ws and a Z in the pool). Then, exchange the FQV. In this way, you will give your opponent at least one awkward letter, or maybe even all three. Let the letters cause him some problems. Make the letters work for you, even if it's only being left on your opponent's rack at the end of the game. Of course, if you do put back three tiles, you could get one or two of them back. You have put back FQV and picked up EEE, say; your opponent plays one letter, and picks up the Q, say; you play a letter, and then pick up the F; and your opponent plays one letter, and picks up the final V. You have at least managed to dump two of your three unwanted letters onto your opponent. One thing: Don't be timid about exchanging right at the end of the game. Your opponent would probably do it to you given half the chance; and if he wouldn't do it to you, he deserves to have it done to him, anyway!

If you decide to return awkward letters to the pool near the end of the game, be careful not to put them back too soon. The more tiles you return and the sooner you do it, the greater are your chances of getting them back again.

If you decide against exchanging any letters at the end of a game, you must make your end-game plays the best possible, and these are not necessarily the ones scoring the most points. Consider this example. You have ADDFOYZ on your rack, and your opponent has just one letter on his. He is almost certain to go out on his next turn. You might be able to make DYAD and some other words for the total of 30 points, or FOZY for only 21 points. But FOZY is the better move. Why? If your opponent goes out on his next turn, he will catch you holding ADD (worth 5 points). That's five points added to his score, and five points deducted from your score. This means that you have made a net score of 11 points. (That is, 21 points minus 5 points twice.) But had you played DYAD for 30 points, and then your opponent had gone out, he would catch you for 15 points, with FOZ on your rack. He will get 15 points added to his score, and you will get 15 points deducted from yours. The net value to you is zero points. (That is, 30 points minus 15 points twice.) Thus, FOZY is worth 11 points more to you than DYAD, even though it actually scores 9 points *less* when it is played!

SUMMARY

Players are basically of two types, defensive and offensive. How a particular game turns out will depend on your personality, that of your opponent, and what each of you perceives the object of the game to be. Is it to win? Is it to win and score highly? Is it to score highly? If winning is all-important, a player may be quite happy to finish with 250 points against his opponent's 240 points. If you want to score highly as well, you may be dissatisfied with any win that doesn't score at least 450 points. A win of 500 points to 400 will please you; a win of 410 to 400 won't please you. Other players have another objective, merely to enjoy the game. But the very best players somehow manage to combine all three objectives. They win, they score highly, and they enjoy the game.

If you aim only to win, regardless of what the final scores are, you best bet is a defensive game. In such a game, players tend to use lots of short words and lots of tightly interlocking words. They open up very little of the board, hoping to stop their opponent from scoring highly. If the opponent attempts to make an opening for himself, that is likely to be blocked quickly. A defensive player will avoid opening up the more valuable premium squares. However, while a defensive player is trying to make life difficult for his opponent, he must try to avoid giving himself a hard time. This is where many inexperienced defensive players go wrong. They often end up with exactly the same problems

FIGURE 43

that their opponent has. Good defensive play is an art, just as is good offensive play. But it can be more easily achieved and is usually less elegant than good offensive play. The words played in a defensive game are often clustered in just one half of the board, any opportunity of using the other half of the board having been largely eliminated. *Figure 43* is an example of a partly finished defensive game. There is only a slim chance of this game expanding to the other half of the board. Many inexperienced players find themselves in this situation quite by accident, having successfully managed to thwart their opponent's play as well as their own! It takes a good player to get the best from such tight situations.

An offensive player goes all out for 50-point bonuses. He runs risks, and he opens up premium score squares, especially triple-word-score squares, for his opponent, in the hope that the board will quickly be opened up even further, giving him plenty of opportunities to get his bonus words down. Good offensive play tends to be quite elegant. A good player will hop about the board, using a premium square here, opening up a premium square there, and collecting four or five bonuses in the process. The bonuses will have sandwiched between them quite a few intermediate scores, in the 25–40 points range. Of course, an offensive player doesn't just open up any old premium squares for his opponent. There will be times when he just cannot afford to do this. If he knows that his opponent has a blank on his rack, there is no point in handing him a place to put his bonus word that gets tripled in the process.

If an opponent is not an accomplished player, he may be unable to take advantage of the premium squares offered him, so the "carrots" being dangled in front of him are wasted, but they can then be used by the more experienced player. On the other hand, two very experienced players, both fully aware of each other's vocabulary, style, temperament, and capabilities, will often play a lot less offensively against each other than they would against lesser players. They know only too well that any premium squares opened up are likely to be promptly and effectively used, but with no new premium squares being opened up as a result. *Figure 44* illustrates a particularly open and high-scoring game, the product of some good offensive play. (The letters EK remained unplayed at the end of the game, and the blanks were used as the U of CONQUERS and the T of BARONETS.)

FIGURE 44

SCRABBLE® BRAND CROSSWORD GAME PLAYERS RECORDS AND HIGH SCORES

Players are always inquiring what the highest possible score for a single move is. Or what the highest actual score for a complete game is. Or how long was the longest game. And so on. A number of records are described here.

Here are the records and high scores.

Highest Theoretical Score

The highest theoretical score is 5,874 points. If you use only words acceptable in the tournament level play in the

U.S. and Canada, the best that you could do is 3,767 points, using *Merriam Webster's New Collegiate Dictionary* and the OSPD, or 2,354 points, using only words listed in the OSPD. This was devised by Steven C. Root of Westboro, Massachusetts.

Highest Single Turn

The highest single turn with OSPD words is MAXIMIZING for 613 points. This was devised by Kyle Corbin of Raleigh, North Carolina.

Maximum Score for One Tile

The maximum score for one tile is 213, using standard American dictionaries, or 165 with the OSPD listings. Devised by Kyle Corbin of Raleigh, North Carolina.

World Records

Whether SESQUIOXIDIZING for 2,069 points or BENZOXYCAMPHORS for 1,593 are world records depends on how you interpret rule 8 of Scrabble® brand crossword game. With unabridged dictionaries they are possible (the 1967 revision permits them). With standard desk dictionaries, the type of lexicon originally specified in the game's rules, the best would be Kyle Corbin's 1,682, building on DEMYTHOLOGIZERS, which appears in *Merriam Webster's New Collegiate Dictionary*.

Highest Tournament Score in the U.S.

The highest tournament score in the U.S. was achieved by Chris Reslock, an East Lansing, Michigan, taxi driver. His 719–221 win in Greene County, Ohio, in 1980 set the record.

Highest Tournament Score in Canada

Mike Krepakevich of Toronto, Canada, holds the formal Canadian record (666–329).

Highest Tournament Score in Australia

John Holgate has the top score (728–295) in official competitions in Australia.

Reigning North American Champion

The reigning champion is Joel Wapnick, a music professor at McGill University in Montreal, Canada. He will defend his crown in August 1985. Previous champions were David Prinz in 1978 and Joseph Edley in 1980, both from San Francisco, California.

Highest Score on the First Move

The highest theoretical scores, with different numbers of letters, that can be achieved on the very first move in a game are as follows:

2 letters– AX, EX, OX, XI, XU, JO (18 points). This is in the OSPD.

3 letters– ZAX (38 points). This is in the OSPD.

4 letters– QUIZ (44 points). This is in the OSPD.

5 letters– SQUIZ (66 points). This is a glance, or a look, and can be found in *Webster's Third New International Dictionary*. The highest-scoring words from the OSPD are JAZZY, QUAKY, ZINKY, and ZIPPY, all being worth 62 points. Note that it is necessary to use a blank as a Z in JAZZY.

6 letters– QUEAZY (74 points). This is in the OSPD.

7 letters– ZYXOMMA (130 points). This is *not* in the OSPD. It is a type of Indian dragonfly, and can be found in Funk and Wagnall's *New Standard Dictionary*. The highest-scoring words from the OSPD are JUKEBOX, QUIZZED, SQUEEZE, and ZYMURGY, scoring 120 points each.

Highest Score for First Two Moves

The highest theoretical score that can be achieved in the first two moves of a game is 348 points. The first player puts down QUIZZER for 118 points, with the Q on the center square and the first Z represented by a blank. QUIZZER is in the OSPD. The second player plays HYDROXY perpendicular to QUIZZER, making QUIZZERY. The first Y of HYDROXY and the Y of QUIZZERY are represented by the same tile. This scores 230 points. HYDROXY is in the OSPD. QUIZZERY is not in the OSPD, but is in *The Oxford English Dictionary*. The total score for these first two moves is 348 points.

Highest Real Score in a Single Move

The highest known score achieved at a single move in a real game is 392 points. This was achieved by playing the word CAZIQUES across two triple-word-score squares, and getting the Q on a double-letter-score square. This score was made by Dr. Karlo Khoshnaw, of Manchester, England, on April 11th, 1982.

Highest Real Game Score

The highest known score achieved by one player in a real game is 774 points. This was achieved by Allan Simmons of London, England, on July 1st, 1981.

Most Bonuses in a Real Game

The highest number of 50-point bonuses in a real game is 7. This was achieved by Darryl Francis, of Wandsworth, London, on March 9th, 1974. Mr. Francis's total score at the end of the game was 656 points.

Highest Idealized Score in a Single Move

In an idealized game, the highest score yet discovered for *one single move* is 1,961 points. This idealized move was devised by Ron Jerome, of Bracknell, Berkshire, England, in

May 1974. The move involved playing all seven tiles, combining them with eight already on the board, to form a fifteen-letter word, that stretched across three triple-word-score squares. As well as making this fifteen-letter word, the move also created seven words perpendicular to it, three stretching across triple-word-score squares.

The fifteen-letter word that was played was BENZOXY-CAMPHORS. The seven other words were DAFFODILLY, GULLISH, JINNYRICKSHAWS, PROVERB, SQUANDERMA-NIAC, VAGABONDAGER, and WERTUZ. (The words DAFFO-DILL, GULLIS, JINNYRICKSHAW, PROVER, SQUANDERMA-NIA, VAGABONDAGE, and WERTU were already on the board.)

Where can all these strange words be found?

BENZOXYCAMPHORS—*Webster's New International Dictionary*, Second Edition

DAFFODILL—*Oxford English Dictionary*

DAFFODILLY—*Webster's Third New International Dictionary*

GULLIS—*Oxford English Dictionary*

GULLISH—*Webster's Third New International Dictionary*

JINNYRICKSHAW(S)—*Oxford English Dictionary*

PROVER—The OSPD

PROVERB—The OSPD

SQUANDERMANIA—*Webster's Third New International Dictionary*

SQUANDERMANIAC—*Webster's New International Dictionary*, Second Edition

VAGABONDAGE—*Webster's Third New International Dictionary*

VAGABONDAGER—*Oxford English Dictionary*

WERTU—*Oxford English Dictionary*

WERTUZ—*Oxford English Dictionary*

Highest Idealized Game Score
In an idealized game, the highest final score for one player that has yet been discovered is 4,153 points. This idealized game was devised by Ralph Beaman, of Pennsylvania, in 1974.

Longest Continuous Play of Games
The longest game lasted 120 hours. This was achieved by Norman Hazeldean, Alan Giles, Tom Barton, and Keith Ollett, at Uckfield, East Sussex, England, from August 4th to 9th, 1975.

4
VOCABULARY

The essential lists of words that will enable a player to become a true master of the game.

TWO-LETTER WORDS

This is a complete list of the two-letter words that are in *The Official Scrabble® Players Dictionary.*

Next to each word is (1) an abbreviation indicating the word's part of speech (adj = adjective, adv = adverb, int = interjection, n = noun, prep = preposition, pron = pronoun, and vb = verb), and (2) a brief meaning for the word.

Meanings are given to help the reader fix a word in his mind. It is usually the case that a word is more easily remembered if it has some meaning associated with it. It is then more than a sequence of letters.

Word	Part of Speech	Meaning
AA	n	rough cindery lava
AD	n	an advertisement
AE	adj	one
AH	int	expressing delight
AI	n	the three-toed sloth
AM	vb	first person singular of the verb "to be"
AN	adj	indefinite article
AR	n	the letter R
AS	adv	to the same degree
AT	prep	in the position of
AW	int	expressing protest

Word	Part of Speech	Meaning
AX	vb	to cut down
AY	n	an affirmative vote
BA	n	the eternal soul
BE	vb	to exist
BI	n	a bisexual
BO	n	a pal
BY	prep	near to
DA	prep	of, from
DE	prep	of, from
DO	vb	to perform
EF	n	the letter F
EH	int	expressing doubt
EL	n	an elevated railroad
EM	n	the letter M
EN	n	the letter N
ER	int	expressing hesitation
ES	n	the letter S
ET	vb	past tense of "to eat"
EX	n	the letter X
FA	n	a musical note
GO	vb	to move along
HA	n	a sound of surprise
HE	n	a male person
HI	int	used as a greeting
HO	int	expressing surprise
ID	n	part of the psyche
IF	n	a possibility
IN	vb	to harvest
IS	vb	part of the verb "to be"
IT	pron	the neuter form of "he" and "him"
JO	n	a sweetheart
KA	n	the spiritual self
LA	n	a musical note

Word	Part of Speech	Meaning
LI	n	a Chinese unit of distance
LO	int	expressing surprise
MA	n	mother
ME	pron	objective case of the pronoun "I"
MI	n	a musical note
MU	n	a Greek letter
MY	pron	possessive form of the pronoun "I"
NA	adv	no
NO	n	a negative reply
NU	n	a Greek letter
OD	n	a type of force
OE	n	a whirlwind
OF	prep	coming from
OH	vb	to exclaim in surprise
OM	n	a mantra
ON	n	the side of the wicket where the batsman stands in cricket
OP	n	a style of art
OR	n	the tincture gold
OS	n	a bone
OW	int	expressing pain
OX	n	a hoofed mammal
OY	int	expressing dismay
PA	n	father
PE	n	a Hebrew letter
PI	n	a Greek letter
RE	n	a musical note
SH	int	urging silence
SI	n	a musical note
SO	n	a musical note
TA	n	an expression of gratitude
TI	n	a musical note
TO	prep	in the direction of

Word	Part of Speech	Meaning
UN	pron	one
UP	vb	to raise
US	pron	the objective case of the pronoun "we"
UT	n	a musical note
WE	pron	the plural of the pronoun "I"
WO	n	woe
XI	n	a Greek letter
XU	n	monetary unit of Vietnam
YA	pron	you
YE	pron	you

THREE-LETTER WORDS

This is a complete list of the three-letter words that are in *The Official Scrabble® Players Dictionary,* or are plural or verb forms (created by the addition of an S) of two-letter words in the dictionary.

The words have been split into four groups. Group I is composed of words where the first two letters and the last two letters of each word are both two-letter words (for example, ADO is composed of both AD and DO); group II is composed of words where only the last two letters of each word form a two-letter word (for example, AGO has only its last two letters making a word, GO; AG is not an allowable two-letter word); group III is composed of words where only the first two letters of each word form a two-letter word (for example, ADD has only its first two letters making a word, AD; DD is not, of course, an allowable two-letter word); and group IV is composed of words where neither the first two letters nor the last two letters of each word form a two-letter word (for example, in the word ACE, neither AC nor CE is an allowable two-letter word).

Group I

AAH	BOW	HAD	LAT
AAS	BOX	HAE	LAW
ADO	BOY	HAH	LAX
AHA	BYE	HAM	LAY
AID	DAD	HAS	LID
AIN	DAH	HAT	LIN
AIS	DAM	HAW	LIS
AIT	DAW	HAY	LIT
AMA	DAY	HEM	LOP
AMI	DEL	HEN	LOW
AMU	DEN	HER	LOX
ANA	DES	HES	MAD
ARE	DEX	HET	MAE
ASH	DOE	HEX	MAN
AWE	DOM	HID	MAR
AYE	DON	HIN	MAS
BAA	DOR	HIS	MAT
BAD	DOS	HIT	MAW
BAH	DOW	HOD	MAY
BAN	EME	HOE	MEL
BAR	EMU	HOP	MEM
BAS	ERE	HOW	MEN
BAT	ETA	HOY	MET
BAY	FAD	JOE	MID
BEL	FAN	JOW	MIS
BEN	FAR	JOY	MUN
BET	FAS	KAE	MUS
BID	FAT	KAS	MUT
BIN	FAX	KAT	NAE
BIS	FAY	KAY	NAY
BIT	GOD	LAD	NOD
BOD	GOR	LAM	NOH
BOP	GOX	LAR	NOM
BOS	GOY	LAS	NOR

NOS	PEN	SOX	TOY
NOW	PER	SOY	UTA
NUN	PES	TAD	WEN
NUS	PET	TAE	WET
NUT	PIN	TAM	WOE
ODE	PIS	TAN	WON
OES	PIT	TAR	WOP
OHO	REF	TAS	WOS
OPE	REM	TAT	WOW
ORE	RES	TAW	XIS
OWE	RET	TAX	YAH
PAD	REX	TIN	YAM
PAH	SHE	TIS	YAR
PAM	SIN	TIT	YAW
PAN	SIS	TOD	YAY
PAR	SIT	TOE	YEH
PAS	SOD	TOM	YEN
PAT	SON	TON	YES
PAW	SOP	TOP	YET
PAX	SOS	TOR	
PAY	SOW	TOW	

Group II

ABA	CAN	COX	EAT
ABO	CAR	COY	EEL
ABY	CAT	CUP	EGO
AGO	CAW	CUT	EON
ALA	CAY	DID	EWE
APE	CHI	DIN	EYE
BUN	COD	DIT	FEN
BUS	CON	DUN	FER
BUT	COP	DUP	FET
CAD	COS	DYE	FID
CAM	COW	EAR	FIN

FIT	JET	POD	SEN
FOE	JIN	POH	SER
FOH	JUN	POP	SET
FON	JUS	POW	SEX
FOP	JUT	POX	SPA
FOR	KEF	PSI	SUN
FOX	KEN	PUN	SUP
FOY	KEX	PUP	TEN
FUN	KHI	PUS	THE
GAD	KID	PUT	THO
GAE	KIF	PYA	TUN
GAM	KIN	PYE	TUP
GAN	KIT	RAD	TUT
GAR	KOP	RAH	TWO
GAS	KOR	RAM	TYE
GAT	KOS	RAN	UDO
GAY	LET	RAS	UIT
GEL	LEX	RAT	VAN
GEM	LYE	RAW	VAS
GET	MHO	RAX	VAT
GHI	MOD	RAY	VAW
GID	MOM	RHO	VET
GIN	MON	RID	VEX
GIT	MOP	RIN	VIN
GNU	MOR	ROD	VIS
GUN	MOW	ROE	VOE
GUT	NET	ROW	VON
HUN	NIT	RUN	VOW
HUP	OAR	RUT	VOX
HUT	OAT	RYA	WAD
ION	OBE	RYE	WAE
IRE	OBI	SAD	WAN
JAM	OKA	SAE	WAR
JAR	OOH	SAT	WAS
JAW	OUT	SAU	WAT
JAY	PHI	SEL	WAW

WAX	WIN	YID	YON
WAY	WIS	YIN	YOW
WHA	WIT	YOD	YUP
WHO	WYE	YOM	ZAX

Group III

AAL	BAG	DOT	HAP
ADD	BAL	EFF	HEP
ADS	BED	EFS	HEW
ADZ	BEE	EFT	HEY
AIL	BEG	ELD	HIC
AIM	BEY	ELF	HIE
AIR	BIB	ELK	HIM
AMP	BIG	ELL	HIP
AND	BIO	ELM	HOB
ANE	BOA	ELS	HOG
ANI	BOB	EMS	HOT
ANT	BOG	END	IDS
ANY	BOO	ENG	IFS
ARC	BOT	ENS	INK
ARF	BYS	ERA	INN
ARK	DAB	ERG	INS
ARM	DAG	ERN	ISM
ARS	DAK	ERR	ITS
ART	DAP	ERS	JOB
ASK	DEB	ESS	JOG
ASP	DEE	ETH	JOT
ASS	DEI	FAG	KAB
ATE	DEV	GOA	LAB
AWA	DEW	GOB	LAC
AWL	DEY	GOO	LAG
AWN	DOC	GOT	LAP
AXE	DOG	HAG	LIB
AYS	DOL	HAJ	LIE

114

LIP	OFF	PIC	TAO
LOB	OFT	PIE	TAP
LOG	OHM	PIG	TAU
LOO	OHS	PIP	TAV
LOT	OMS	PIU	TIC
MAC	ONE	PIX	TIE
MAG	ONS	REB	TIL
MAP	OPS	REC	TIP
MEW	OPT	RED	TOG
MIB	ORA	REE	TOO
MIG	ORB	REI	TOT
MIL	ORC	REP	UNS
MIM	ORS	REV	UPO
MIR	ORT	SHH	UPS
MIX	OSE	SHY	USE
MUD	OWL	SIB	UTS
MUG	OWN	SIC	WEB
MUM	OXY	SIM	WED
NAB	PAC	SIP	WEE
NAG	PAL	SIR	WOK
NAP	PAP	SIX	WOO
NOB	PEA	SOB	WOT
NOG	PED	SOL	YAK
NOO	PEE	SOT	YAP
NOT	PEG	SOU	YEA
NUB	PEP	TAB	YEP
ODD	PEW	TAG	YEW
ODS	PIA	TAJ	

Group IV

ACE	AGA	ALL	AUK
ACT	AGE	ALP	AVA
AFF	ALB	ALT	AVE
AFT	ALE	APT	AVO

AZO	DUO	GED	KEP
BRA	EAU	GEE	KEY
BUB	EBB	GEY	KIP
BUD	ECU	GIB	KOA
BUG	EDH	GIE	KUE
BUM	EGG	GIG	LEA
BUR	EKE	GIP	LED
BUY	EVE	GUL	LEE
CAB	FED	GUM	LEG
CAP	FEE	GUY	LEI
CEE	FEU	GYM	LEK
COB	FEW	GYP	LEU
COG	FEY	HUB	LEV
COL	FEZ	HUE	LEY
COO	FIB	HUG	LUG
COT	FIE	HUH	LUM
COZ	FIG	HUM	LUX
CRY	FIL	HYP	MOA
CUB	FIR	ICE	MOB
CUD	FIX	ICH	MOG
CUE	FIZ	ICY	MOL
CUM	FLU	ILK	MOO
CUR	FLY	ILL	MOT
CWM	FOB	IMP	NEB
DIB	FOG	IRK	NEE
DIE	FOU	IVY	NEW
DIG	FRO	JAB	NIB
DIM	FRY	JAG	NIL
DIP	FUB	JEE	NIM
DRY	FUD	JEU	NIP
DUB	FUG	JEW	NIX
DUC	FUR	JIB	NTH
DUD	GAB	JIG	OAF
DUE	GAG	JUG	OAK
DUG	GAL	KEA	OCA
DUI	GAP	KEG	OIL

116

OKE	RIM	SRI	VEG
OLD	RIP	STY	VIA
OLE	ROB	SUB	VIE
OOT	ROC	SUE	VIM
OUD	ROT	SUM	VUG
OUR	RUB	TEA	WAB
OVA	RUE	TED	WAG
PHT	RUG	TEE	WAP
PLY	RUM	TEG	WHY
POI	SAB	TEW	WIG
POL	SAC	THY	WIZ
POT	SAG	TRY	WRY
PRO	SAL	TSK	WUD
PRY	SAP	TUB	YIP
PUB	SAW	TUG	YOU
PUD	SAX	TUI	YUK
PUG	SAY	TUX	ZAG
PUL	SEA	TWA	ZAP
PUR	SEC	UGH	ZED
PYX	SEE	UKE	ZEE
QUA	SEI	UMP	ZIG
RAG	SEW	URD	ZIP
RAJ	SKI	URN	ZOA
RAP	SKY	VAU	ZOO
RIB	SLY	VAV	
RIG	SPY	VEE	

FOUR-LETTER AND FIVE-LETTER WORDS WITH
HIGH-VALUE LETTERS

This is a list of four-letter and five-letter words having a J, Q, X, or Z. All the words are in *The Official Scrabble® Players Dictionary.*

Generally, plurals and verb forms of two-, three-, and four-letter words have been omitted from these lists.

FOUR-LETTER WORDS WITH HIGH-VALUE LETTERS

J

AJAR	JAUK	JIFF	JOUK
AJEE	JAUP	JILL	JOWL
DOJO	JAVA	JILT	JUBA
FUJI	JAZZ	JIMP	JUBE
HADJ	JEAN	JINK	JUDO
HAJI	JEEP	JINN	JUGA
HAJJ	JEER	JINX	JUJU
JACK	JEEZ	JIVE	JUKE
JADE	JEFE	JOCK	JUMP
JAGG	JEHU	JOEY	JUNK
JAIL	JELL	JOHN	JUPE
JAKE	JERK	JOIN	JURA
JAMB	JESS	JOKE	JURY
JANE	JEST	JOLE	JUST
JAPE	JETE	JOLT	JUTE
JARK	JEUX	JOSH	RAJA
JARL	JIBB	JOSS	SOJA
JATO	JIBE	JOTA	

Q

QAID	QUAG	QUEY	QUIT
QOPH	QUAI	QUID	QUIZ
QUAD	QUAY	QUIP	QUOD

X

APEX	EXAM	JINX	OXIM
AXAL	EXEC	LUXE	PIXY
AXEL	EXIT	LYNX	PREX
AXIL	EXPO	MAXI	ROUX
AXIS	FIXT	MINX	SEXT
AXLE	FLAX	MIXT	SEXY
AXON	FLEX	MOXA	TAXA
BOXY	FLUX	NEXT	TAXI
CALX	FOXY	NIXY	TEXT
COAX	HOAX	ONYX	VEXT
COXA	IBEX	ORYX	WAXY
COXY	ILEX	OXEN	XYST
CRUX	IXIA	OXES	
DOXY	JEUX	OXID	

Z

ADZE	GAZE	PHIZ	ZEST
AZAN	HAZE	QUIZ	ZETA
AZON	HAZY	RAZE	ZINC
BUZZ	IZAR	RAZZ	ZING
CHEZ	JAZZ	RITZ	ZITI
COZY	LAZE	SIZE	ZOEA
CZAR	LAZY	SIZY	ZOIC
DAZE	MAZE	TZAR	ZONE
DOZE	MAZY	WHIZ	ZOOM
DOZY	MOZO	ZANY	ZOON
FIZZ	NAZI	ZARF	ZORI
FOZY	OOZE	ZEAL	ZYME
FRIZ	OOZY	ZEBU	
FUZE	OUZO	ZEIN	
FUZZ	OYEZ	ZERO	

FIVE-LETTER WORDS WITH HIGH-VALUE LETTERS

J

AJIVA	JAPAN	JIMPY	JUMBO
BANJO	JAPER	JINGO	JUMPY
BIJOU	JAUNT	JINNI	JUNCO
DJINN	JAWAN	JOCKO	JUNKY
ENJOY	JAZZY	JOINT	JUNTA
FJELD	JEBEL	JOIST	JUNTO
FJORD	JEHAD	JOKER	JUPON
GANJA	JELLY	JOLLY	JURAL
HADJI	JEMMY	JOLTY	JURAT
HAJJI	JENNY	JORAM	JUREL
JABOT	JERID	JORUM	JUROR
JACAL	JERKY	JOTTY	JUTTY
JACKY	JERRY	JOULE	KOPJE
JAGER	JESSE	JOUST	MAJOR
JAGGY	JETON	JUDAS	MUJIK
JAGRA	JETTY	JUDGE	RAJAH
JAKES	JEWEL	JUGAL	SAJOU
JALAP	JIBER	JUGUM	SHOJI
JALOP	JIFFY	JUICE	
JAMBE	JIHAD	JUICY	
JANTY	JIMMY	JULEP	

Q

EQUAL	QUAKY	QUASS	QUEST
EQUIP	QUALM	QUATE	QUEUE
MAQUI	QUANT	QUEAN	QUICK
PIQUE	QUARE	QUEEN	QUIET
QUACK	QUARK	QUEER	QUIFF
QUAFF	QUART	QUELL	QUILL
QUAIL	QUASH	QUERN	QUILT
QUAKE	QUASI	QUERY	QUINT

QUIPU	QUOIN	QURSH	SQUAW
QUIRE	QUOIT	ROQUE	SQUIB
QUIRK	QUOTA	SQUAB	SQUID
QUIRT	QUOTE	SQUAD	TOQUE
QUITE	QUOTH	SQUAT	TUQUE

X

ADDAX	EPOXY	MIXER	SIXTY
ADMIX	EXACT	MIXUP	TAXER
AFFIX	EXALT	MOXIE	TAXON
ANNEX	EXCEL	MUREX	TAXUS
ATAXY	EXERT	NEXUS	TELEX
AUXIN	EXILE	NIXIE	TEXAS
AXIAL	EXINE	OXBOW	TOXIC
AXILE	EXIST	OXEYE	TOXIN
AXIOM	EXPEL	OXIDE	UNFIX
AXITE	EXTOL	OXIME	UNSEX
AXMAN	EXTRA	OXLIP	VARIX
AXONE	EXUDE	OXTER	VEXER
BEAUX	EXULT	PHLOX	VEXIL
BORAX	EXURB	PIXIE	VIXEN
BOXER	FIXER	PREXY	WAXEN
BRAXY	FLAXY	PROXY	WAXER
BUXOM	HELIX	PYXIE	XEBEC
CALIX	HEXAD	PYXIS	XENIA
CALYX	HYRAX	RADIX	XENIC
CAREX	INDEX	REDOX	XENON
CODEX	INFIX	RELAX	XERIC
COXAE	IXTLE	REMEX	XERUS
COXAL	KYLIX	SILEX	XYLEM
CULEX	LATEX	SIXMO	XYLAN
CYLIX	LAXLY	SIXTE	XYLOL
DIXIT	MAXIM	SIXTH	XYLYL

Z

ABUZZ	DIAZO	JAZZY	UNZIP
AGAZE	DIZZY	KAZOO	VIZIR
AMAZE	DOZEN	KLUTZ	VIZOR
AZIDE	DOZER	KUDZU	WALTZ
AZIDO	FEEZE	LAZAR	WHIZZ
AZINE	FEZES	MAIZE	WINZE
AZOIC	FIZZY	MATZA	WIZEN
AZOLE	FRIZZ	MATZO	WOOZY
AZOTE	FROZE	MAZER	ZAIRE
AZOTH	FURZE	MEZZO	ZAMIA
AZURE	FURZY	MIZEN	ZANZA
BAIZA	FUZEE	MUZZY	ZAYIN
BAIZE	FUZIL	NERTZ	ZEBEC
BAZAR	FUZZY	NIZAM	ZEBRA
BEZEL	GAUZE	OUZEL	ZESTY
BEZIL	GAUZY	OZONE	ZIBET
BLAZE	GAZER	PIZZA	ZILCH
BLITZ	GHAZI	PLAZA	ZINCY
BONZE	GIZMO	PRIZE	ZINGY
BOOZE	GLAZE	RAZEE	ZINKY
BOOZY	GLAZY	RAZER	ZIPPY
BRAZA	GLOZE	RAZOR	ZIRAM
BRAZE	GRAZE	RITZY	ZLOTY
CLOZE	HAFIZ	SEIZE	ZOEAE
COLZA	HAMZA	SIZAR	ZOEAL
COZEN	HAZAN	SIZER	ZOMBI
COZEY	HAZEL	SPITZ	ZONAL
COZIE	HAZER	TAZZA	ZOOID
CRAZE	HEEZE	TAZZE	ZORIL
CRAZY	HERTZ	TIZZY	
CROZE	HUZZA	TOPAZ	

SOME SEVEN-LETTER WORDS LISTS

This section contains fifty lists of seven-letter words. Each list is headed by a group of six common letters (for example, AENRST, AGINST, DEINRS, and EGILNS). Beneath each heading and in order are the twenty-six letters of the alphabet. If any of the twenty-six letters plus the six-letter heading can be rearranged to form a seven-letter word, then this will be shown. If more than one seven-letter word can be made, they will be shown. For example, on the AENRST list, it can be seen that AENRST plus an A does not make a seven-letter word, so none is shown next to the A on that list; but AENRST plus the letter B makes BANTERS, and this is shown next to the B on that list; better still, AENRST plus the letter C makes several seven-letter words, and these are all shown next to the C on the list. And so on through the alphabet. All of the words in these lists are in *The Official Scrabble® Players Dictionary.*

You will find it instructive to browse through these lists, learning which letters do and don't go with the various six-letter groups. If you are holding AEILNR and then pick a D as your seventh tile, you may be convinced that you have a word, and, like countless other players before you, you may waste a great deal of time trying to find it. Once you have become familiar with these lists, though, you will know instantly that ADEILNR does not form an allowable Scrabble® word. (IRELAND, of course, is a proper name, and it isn't in the dictionary, anyway.) You can then begin to decide which letters to play or return to the pool of unused letters.

Though there are fifty lists here, many others could have been produced. Enthusiastic readers might like to compile their own lists. Some six-letter groups that are likely to be worth investigating are these: ADEILR, ADEILT, ADEINR, ADEIRT, ADENRT, AEELRT, AEELST, AEGINT, DEINST, EEINRS, EEINRT, and EEINST.

ACGINR		ADEILS	
A		A	
B	BRACING	B	DISABLE
C		C	SCAILED
D	CARDING	D	LADDIES
E		E	AEDILES
F	FARCING	F	
G	GRACING	G	
H	ARCHING, CHAGRIN, CHARING	H	HALIDES
I		I	DAILIES, LIAISED, SEDILIA
J		J	
K	ARCKING, CARKING, RACKING	K	
		L	DALLIES, SALLIED
		M	MISDEAL, MISLEAD
L		N	DENIALS, SNAILED
M		O	ISOLEAD
N	CRANING	P	ALIPEDS, PALSIED
O	ORGANIC	Q	
P	CARPING, CRAPING	R	DERAILS
Q		S	AIDLESS
R		T	DETAILS, DILATES
S	RACINGS, SCARING	U	AUDILES
T	CARTING, CRATING, TRACING	V	DEVISAL
U		W	
V	CARVING, CRAVING	X	
W		Y	DIALYSE
X		Z	
Y			
Z	CRAZING		

ADEINS		ADEIRS	
A	NAIADES	A	
B	BANDIES	B	BRAISED, DARBIES
C	CANDIES, INCASED	C	RADICES, SIDECAR
D	DANDIES	D	
E	ANISEED	E	DEARIES, READIES
F		F	
G		G	
H		H	SHADIER
I		I	DAIRIES, DIARIES
J		J	
K		K	DAIKERS, DARKIES
L	DENIALS, SNAILED	L	DERAILS
M	MAIDENS, MEDIANS	M	MISREAD, ADMIRES,
N			SEDARIM, SIDEARM
O		N	RANDIES, SANDIER, SARDINE
P	PANDIES	O	
Q		P	ASPIRED, DESPAIR, DIAPERS,
R	RANDIES, SANDIER, SARDINE		PRAISED
S		Q	
T	DETAINS, INSTEAD, SAINTED,	R	RAIDERS
	STAINED	S	
U		T	ARIDEST, ASTRIDE, DISRATE,
V	INVADES		STAIDER, TARDIES, TIRADES
W		U	RESIDUA
X		V	ADVISER
Y		W	
Z		X	RADIXES
		Y	
		Z	

ADEIST

A
B
C
D
E IDEATES
F
G AGISTED
H
I
J
K
L DETAILS, DILATES
M MISDATE
N DETAINS, INSTEAD, SAINTED,
   STAINED
O IODATES, TOADIES
P
Q
R ARIDEST, ASTRIDE, DISRATE,
   STAIDER, TARDIES, TIRADES
S DISSEAT
T
U DAUTIES
V DATIVES
W DAWTIES, WAISTED
X
Y
Z

ADENRS

A
B BANDERS
C DANCERS
D DANDERS
E ENDEARS
F
G DANGERS, GANDERS,
   GARDENS
H HARDENS
I RANDIES, SANDIER, SARDINE
J
K DARKENS
L DARNELS, LANDERS,
   SLANDER, SNARLED
M REMANDS
N
O
P PANDERS
Q
R DARNERS, ERRANDS
S SANDERS
T STANDER
U ASUNDER, DANSEUR
V
W WANDERS, WARDENS
X
Y
Z ZANDERS

AEERST

A   AERATES
B   BEATERS, BERATES, REBATES
C   CERATES, CREATES, ECARTES
D   DEAREST, REDATES, SEDATER
E
F   AFREETS, FEASTER
G   ERGATES, RESTAGE
H   AETHERS, HEATERS, REHEATS
I   SERIATE, AERIEST
J
K   RETAKES
L   ELATERS, REALEST, RELATES,
    STEALER
M   STEAMER
N   EARNEST, EASTERN, NEAREST
O   ROSEATE
P   REPEATS
Q
R   SERRATE, TEARERS
S   RESEATS, SEAREST, TEASERS,
    TESSERA, EASTERS, SEATERS
T   ESTREAT, RESTATE, RETASTE
U   AUSTERE
V
W   SWEATER
X
Y
Z

AEGILN

A
B
C   ANGELIC, ANGLICE
D   ALIGNED, DEALING, LEADING
E   LINEAGE
F   FINAGLE, LEAFING
G
H   HEALING
I
J
K   LEAKING, LINKAGE
L
M
N   ANELING, EANLING, LEANING
O
P   LEAPING, PEALING
Q
R   ENGRAIL, NARGILE, REALIGN,
    REGINAL
S   LEASING, LINAGES, SEALING
T   ATINGLE, ELATING, GELATIN,
    GENITAL
U
V   LEAVING, VEALING
W
X
Y
Z

127

AEGINR		AEGINS	
A		A	
B	BEARING	B	
C		C	CEASING
D	GRADINE, GRAINED,	D	
	READING	E	
E	REGINAE	F	
F	FEARING	G	AGEINGS
G	GEARING	H	
H	HEARING	I	
I		J	
J		K	SINKAGE
K		L	LEASING, LINAGES, SEALING
L	ENGRAIL, NARGILE, REALIGN,	M	ENGIMAS, GAMINES,
	REGINAL		SEAMING
M	GERMINA, MANGIER,	N	
	REAMING	O	AGONIES, AGONISE
N	EARNING, ENGRAIN,	P	SPINAGE
	GRANNIE, NEARING	Q	
O		R	EARINGS, ERASING, GAINERS,
P	REAPING		REGAINS, REGINAS, SEARING,
Q			SERINGA
R	ANGRIER, EARRING, GRAINER,	S	AGNISES
	RANGIER, REARING	T	EASTING, EATINGS, INGATES,
S	EARINGS, ERASING, GAINERS,		INGESTA, SEATING, TEASING
	REGAINS, REGINAS, SEARING,	U	GUINEAS
	SERINGA	V	
T	GRANITE, INGRATE, TANGIER,	W	
	TEARING	X	
U		Y	
V	REAVING, VINEGAR	Z	
W	WEARING		
X			
Y			
Z			

AEGLNS

A	ANLAGES, GALENAS, LASAGNE
B	BANGLES
C	GLANCES
D	DANGLES, LAGENDS, SLANGED
E	
F	FLANGES
G	
H	
I	LEASING, LINAGES, SEALING
J	JANGLES
K	
L	
M	MANGELS, MANGLES
N	
O	
P	SPANGLE
Q	
R	ANGLERS
S	
T	GELANTS, TANGLES
U	ANGELUS, LANGUNES
V	
W	WANGLES
X	
Y	
Z	

AEILNR

A	
B	
C	CARLINE
D	
E	
F	
G	ENGRAIL, NARGILE, REALIGN, REGINAL
H	HERNIAL, INHALER
I	
J	
K	LANKIER
L	RALLINE
M	MANLIER, MARLINE, MINERAL
N	
O	AILERON, ALIENOR
P	PLAINER, PRALINE
Q	
R	
S	ALINERS, NAILERS
T	LATRINE, RATLINE, RELIANT, RETINAL, TRENAIL
U	
V	RAVELIN
W	
X	
Y	INLAYER
Z	

129

AEILRS

A AERIALS
B BAILERS
C CLARIES, ECLAIRS, SCALIER
D DERAILS
E REALISE
F
G GLAIRES
H SHALIER
I SAILIER
J JAILERS
K SERKALI
L RALLIES
M MAILERS, REALISM
N ALINERS, NAILERS
O
P
Q
R RERAILS
S AIRLESS, SAILERS, SERAILS,
   SERIALS
T REALIST, RETAILS, SALTIER,
   SALTIRE, SLATIER, TAILERS
U
V REVISAL
W WAILERS
X
Y
Z

AEILRT

A
B TRIABLE, LIBRATE
C ARTICLE, RECITAL
D DILATER, TRAILED
E ATELIER
F
G
H LATHIER
I
J
K
L LITERAL, TALLIER
M MALTIER
N LATRINE, RATLINE, RELIANT,
   RETINAL, TRENAIL
O
P PLAITER
Q
R RETRIAL, TRAILER
S REALIST, RETAILS, SALTIER,
   SALTIRE, SLATIER, TAILERS
T TERTIAL
U URALITE
V
W
X
Y REALITY
Z

AEILST

A
B ALBITES, BESTIAL, BLASTIE,
   STABILE
C ELASTIC, LACIEST, LATICES
D DETAILS, DILATES
E
F
G AIGLETS, LIGATES
H HALITES
I LAITIES
J
K LAKIEST (see 1st and 2nd
   LAKE), TALKIES
L TAILLES, TALLIES
M
N ELASTIN, ENTAILS, SALIENT,
   TENAILS
O ISOLATE
P PALIEST, TALIPES
Q
R REALIST, RETAILS, SALTIER,
   SALTIRE, SLATIER, TAILERS
S SALTIES
T
U
V
W
X
Y
Z LAZIEST

AEINRS

A
B
C ARSENIC, CARNIES
D RANDIES, SANDIER, SARDINE
E
F INFARES
G EARINGS, ERASING, GAINERS,
   REGAINS, REGINAS, SEARING,
   SERINGA
H HERNIAS
I
J
K SNAKIER
L ALINERS, NAILERS
M MARINES, REMAINS, SEMINAR
N INSANER, INSNARE
O ERASION
P RAPINES
Q
R SIERRAN
S ARSINES
T NASTIER, RATINES, RETAINS,
   RETINAS, RETSINA, STAINER,
   STEARIN
U
V RAVINES
W
X
Y
Z

	AEINRT		AEINST
A		A	TAENIAS
B		B	BASINET
C	CERTAIN	C	CINEAST
D	DETRAIN, TRAINED	D	DETAINS, INSTEAD, SAINTED,
E	RETINAE, TRAINEE		STAINED
F	FAINTER	E	ETESIAN
G	GRANITE, INGRATE, TANGIER,	F	FAINEST
	TEARING	G	EASTING, EATINGS, INGATES,
H	INEARTH		INGESTA, SEATING, TEASING
I	INERTIA	H	
J		I	ISATINE
K	KERATIN	J	
L	LATRINE, RATLINE, RELIANT,	K	INTAKES
	RETINAL, TRENAIL	L	ELASTIN, ENTAILS, NAILSET,
M	MINARET, RAIMENT		SALIENT, SALTINE, TENAILS
N	ENTRAIN	M	ETAMINS, INMATES, TAMEINS
O		N	
P	PAINTER, PERTAIN, REPAINT	O	ATONIES
Q		P	PANTIES, SAPIENT, SPINATE
R	RETRAIN, TERRAIN, TRAINER	Q	
S	NASTIER, RATINES, RETAINS,	R	NASTIER, RATINES, RETAINS,
	RETINAS, RETSINA, STAINER,		RETINAS, RETSINA, STAINER,
	STEARIN		STEARIN
T	INTREAT, ITERANT, NATTIER,	S	ENTASIS, SESTINA, TANSIES,
	NITRATE, TERTIAN		TISANES
U	RUINATE, TAURINE, URANITE,	T	INSTATE, SATINET
	URINATE	U	AUNTIES, SINUATE
V		V	NAIVEST, NATIVES, VAINEST
W	TAWNIER, TINWARE	W	TAWNIES
X		X	
Y		Y	
Z		Z	ZANIEST

AEIRST

A ASTERIA, ATRESIA
B BAITERS, BARITES, REBAITS
C RACIEST, STEARIC
D ARIDEST, ASTRIDE, DISRATE,
   STAIDER, TARDIES, TIRADES
E AERIEST, SERIATE
F FAIREST
G AIGRETS, GAITERS, SEAGIRT,
   STAGIER, TRIAGES
H HASTIER
I AIRIEST
J
K
L REALIST, RETAILS, SALTIER,
   SALTIRE, SLATIER, TAILERS
M MAESTRI, MISRATE, SMARTIE
N NASTIER, RATINES, RETAINS,
   RETINAS, RETSINA, STAINER,
   STEARIN
O
P PARTIES, PASTIER, PIASTER,
   PIASTRE, PIRATES, TRAIPSE
Q
R TARRIES, TARSIER
S SATIRES
T ARTIEST, ARTISTE, ATTIRES,
   STRIATE, TASTIER
U
V VASTIER
W WAISTER, WAITERS, WARIEST
X
Y
Z

AELNRS

A ARSENAL
B
C LANCERS
D DARNELS, LANDERS,
   SLANDER, SNARLED
E
F
G ANGLERS
H
I ALINERS, NAILERS
J
K RANKLES
L
M
N ENSNARL, LANNERS
O LOANERS
P PLANERS, REPLANS
Q
R SNARLER
S
T ANTLERS, RENTALS, SALTERN,
   STERNAL
U
V
W
X
Y
Z

AELNRT		AELNST	
A		A	SEALANT
B		B	
C	CENTRAL	C	CANTLES, CENTALS, LANCETS
D		D	DENTALS, SLANTED
E	ENTERAL, ETERNAL	E	LEANEST
F		F	
G	TANGLER	G	TANGLES
H	ENTHRAL	H	HANTLES
I	LATRINE, RATLINE, RELIANT, RETINAL, TRENAIL	I	ELASTIN, ENTAILS, SALIENT, SALTINE, TENAILS
J		J	
K		K	ANKLETS, LANKEST
L		L	
M		M	LAMENTS, MANTELS, MANTLES
N	LANTERN	N	
O		O	
P	PLANTER, REPLANT	P	PLANETS, PLATENS
Q		Q	
R		R	ANTLERS, RENTALS, SALTERN, STERNAL
S	ANTLERS, RENTALS, SALTERN, STERNAL	S	
T		T	LATTENS, TALENTS
U	NEUTRAL	U	ELUANTS
V	VENTRAL	V	LEVANTS
W		W	
X		X	
Y		Y	
Z		Z	

134

AELRST

A
B BLASTER, LABRETS, STABLER
C CARTELS, CLARETS, SCARLET
D DARTLES
E ELATERS, REALEST, RELATES, STEALER
F FALTERS
G LARGEST
H HALTERS, HARSLET, LATHERS, SLATHER, THALERS
I REALIST, RETAILS, SALTIER, SALTIRE, SLATIER
J
K STALKER, TALKERS
L STELLAR
M ARMLETS, LAMSTER, TRAMELS
N ANTLERS, RENTALS, SALTERN, STERNAL
O
P PALTERS, PERSALT, PLASTER, PLATERS, STAPLER
Q
R
S ARTLESS, LASTERS, SALTERS, SLATERS
T RATTLES, STARLET, STARTLE
U SALUTER
V TRAVELS, VARLETS, VESTRAL
W WASTREL
X
Y
Z

AENRST

A
B BANTERS
C CANTERS, NECTARS, RECANTS, SCANTER, TANRECS, TRANCES
D STANDER
E EARNEST, EASTERN, NEAREST
F
G ARGENTS, GARNETS, STRANGE
H ANTHERS, THENARS
I NASTIER, RATINES, RETAINS, RETINAS, RETSINA, STAINER, STEARIN
J
K RANKEST, TANKERS
L ANTLERS, RENTALS, SALTERN, STERNAL
M MARTENS, SARMENT, SMARTEN
N TANNERS
O ATONERS, SENATOR, TREASON
P ARPENTS, ENTRAPS, PARENTS, PASTERN, TREPANS
Q
R ERRANTS, RANTERS
S
T NATTERS, RATTENS
U NATURES, SAUNTER
V SERVANT, TAVERNS, VERSANT
W WANTERS
X
Y
Z

AEORST		AGHINS	
A		A	
B	BOASTER, BOATERS, BORATES, SORBATE	B	BASHING
		C	CASHING, CHASING
C	COASTER, COATERS	D	DASHING, SHADING
D	ROASTED, TORSADE	E	
E	ROSEATE	F	FASHING
F		G	GASHING
G	ORGEATS, STORAGE	H	HASHING
H	EARSHOT	I	
I		J	
J		K	SHAKING
K		L	LASHING
L		M	MASHING, SHAMING
M	MAESTRO	N	
N	ATONERS, SENATOR, TREASON	O	
		P	HASPING, PHASING, SHAPING
O			
P	ESPARTO, PROTEAS, SEAPORT	Q	
Q		R	GARNISH, SHARING
R	ROASTER	S	SASHING
S		T	HASTING
T	ROTATES, TOASTER	U	ANGUISH
U		V	SHAVING
V		W	SHAWING, WASHING
W		X	
X		Y	HAYINGS
Y		Z	HAZINGS
Z			

	AGINPS		AGINRS
A		A	SANGRIA
B		B	SABRING
C	SCAPING, SPACING	C	RACINGS, SCARING
D	SPADING	D	DARINGS, GRADINS
E	SPAEING, SPINAGE	E	EARINGS, ERASING, GAINERS,
F			REGAINS, REGINAS, SEARING,
G	GASPING		SERINGA
H	HASPING, PHASING,	F	
	SHAPING	G	
I		H	GARNISH, SHARING
J		I	AIRINGS, ARISING, RAISING
K		J	
L	LAPSING, PALINGS, SAPLING	K	
M		L	
N		M	MARGINS
O	SOAPING	N	SNARING
P	SAPPING	O	ORIGANS, SIGNORA,
Q			SOARING
R	PARINGS, PARSING, RASPING,	P	PARINGS, PARSING, RASPING,
	SPARING		SPARING
S	PASSING	Q	
T	PASTING	R	
U	PAUSING	S	
V	PAVINGS	T	RATINGS, STARING
W		U	
X		V	RAVINGS
Y	PAYINGS, SPAYING	W	
Z		X	
		Y	SYRINGA
		Z	

AGINRT		AGINST	
A		A	AGAINST
B		B	BASTING
C	CARTING, CRATING, TRACING	C	ACTINGS, CASTING
D	DARTING, TRADING	D	
E	GRANITE, INGRATE, TANGIER, TEARING	E	EASTING, EATINGS, INGATES, INGESTA, SEATING, TEASING
F	FARTING, RAFTING	F	FASTING
G	GRATING	G	STAGING
H		H	HASTING
I	AIRTING	I	
J		J	
K	KARTING	K	SKATING, STAKING, TAKINGS, TASKING
L		L	LASTING, SALTING, SLATING, STALING
M		M	MASTING, MATINGS
N	RANTING	N	ANTINGS, STANING
O	ORATING	O	AGONIST, GITANOS
P	PARTING, PRATING	P	PASTING
Q		Q	
R	TARRING	R	RATINGS, STARING
S	RATINGS, STARING	S	
T	RATTING	T	STATING, TASTING
U		U	
V		V	STAVING
W		W	TAWSING, WASTING
X		X	
Y		Y	STAYING
Z		Z	

DEENRS

A	ENDEARS
B	BENDERS
C	DECERNS
D	REDDENS
E	NEEDERS, SNEERED
F	FENDERS
G	GENDERS
H	
I	DENIERS, NEREIDS, RESINED
J	
K	
L	LENDERS, SLENDER
M	MENDERS, REMENDS
N	
O	ENDORSE
P	SPENDER
Q	
R	RENDERS
S	REDNESS, RESENDS, SENDERS
T	TENDERS
U	ENDURES, ENSURED
V	VENDERS
W	
X	
Y	
Z	

DEINRS

A	RANDIES, SANDIER, SARDINE
B	BINDERS, REBINDS
C	CINDERS, DISCERN, RESCIND
D	
E	DENIERS, NEREIDS, RESINED
F	FINDERS, FRIENDS, REFINDS
G	ENGIRDS
H	HINDERS, SHRINED
I	INSIDER
J	
K	REDSKIN
L	
M	MINDERS, REMINDS
N	DINNERS, ENDRINS
O	DINEROS, INDORSE, ROSINED, SORDINE
P	PINDERS
Q	
R	
S	
T	TINDERS
U	INSURED
V	
W	REWINDS, WINDERS
X	
Y	
Z	

DEIRST		*EEIRST*	
A	ARIDEST, ASTRIDE, DISRATE, TIRADES	A	AERIEST, SERIATE
B	BESTRID, BISTRED	B	REBITES
C	CREDITS, DIRECTS	C	CERITES, RECITES, TIERCES
D		D	DIETERS
E	DIETERS	E	EERIEST
F		F	
G		G	
H	DITHERS	H	HEISTER
I	DIRTIES	I	
J		J	
K	SKIRTED	K	
L		L	LEISTER, STERILE
M		M	METIERS, TRISEME
N	TINDERS	N	ENTIRES, ENTRIES, TRIENES
O	EDITORS, SORTIED, STEROID, STORIED, TRIODES	O	
P	SPIRTED, STRIPED	P	RESPITE
Q		Q	
R	STIRRED	R	RETIRES, RETRIES, TERRIES
S	STRIDES	S	
T		T	TESTIER
U	DUSTIER, STUDIER	U	
V	DIVERTS, STRIVED	V	RESTIVE, VERIEST
W		W	
X		X	
Y		Y	
Z		Z	ZESTIER

EENRST

A	EARNEST, EASTERN, NEAREST
B	
C	CENTERS, CENTRES, TENRECS
D	TENDERS
E	ENTREES, RETENES
F	
G	GERENTS, REGENTS
H	
I	ENTIRES, ENTRIES, TRENISE
J	
K	
L	RELENTS
M	
N	RENNETS, TENNERS, (see TEN)
O	
P	PRESENT, REPENTS, SERPENT
Q	
R	RENTERS, STERNER
S	RESENTS
T	TENTERS
U	NEUTERS, TENURES, TUREENS
V	VENTERS
W	WESTERN
X	EXTERNS
Y	STYRENE, YESTERN
Z	

EGILNS

A	LEASING, LINAGES, SEALING
B	
C	
D	DINGLES, SINGLED
E	SEELING
F	SELFING
G	LEGGINS, NIGGLES, SNIGGLE
H	SHINGLE
I	
J	JINGLES
K	
L	SELLING
M	MINGLES
N	
O	ELOIGNS, LEGIONS, LINGOES
P	
Q	
R	LINGERS, SLINGER
S	SINGLES
T	GLISTEN, SINGLET, TINGLES
U	
V	
W	SLEWING, SWINGLE
X	
Y	
Z	

EGILNT

A ATINGLE, ELATING, GELATIN, GENITAL
B BELTING
C
D GLINTED, TINGLED
E GENTILE
F FELTING
G
H LIGHTEN
I LIGNITE
J
K KINGLET
L TELLING
M MELTING
N
O LENTIGO
P PELTING
Q
R RINGLET, TINGLER
S GLISTEN, SINGLET, TINGLES
T LETTING
U ELUTING
V
W WELTING, WINGLET
X
Y
Z

EGINRS

A EARINGS, ERASING, GAINERS, REGAINS, REGINAS, SEARING, SERINGA
B
C CRINGES
D ENGIRDS
E GREISEN
F FINGERS, FRINGES
G GINGERS, NIGGERS, SNIGGER
H
I
J
K
L LINGERS, SLINGER
M
N GINNERS
O ERINGOS, IGNORES, REGIONS, SIGNORE
P PINGERS, SPRINGE
Q
R RINGERS
S INGRESS, RESIGNS, SIGNERS, SINGERS
T RESTING, STINGER
U REUSING
V SERVING, VERSING
W SWINGER, WINGERS
X
Y SYRINGE
Z

EGINRT

A   GRANITE, INGRATE, TANGIER,
      TEARING
B
C
D
E   INTEGER, TREEING
F
G
H
I   IGNITER, TIERING
J
K
L   RINGLET, TINGLER
M   METRING, TERMING
N   RENTING, RINGENT
O   GENITOR
P
Q
R
S   RESTING, STINGER
T   GITTERN, RETTING
U   TRUEING
V
W
X
Y
Z

EGINST

A   EASTING, EATINGS, INGATES,
      INGESTA, SEATING, TEASING
B   BESTING
C
D   NIDGETS
E
F
G
H   NIGHEST
I   IGNITES
J   JESTING
K
L   GLISTEN, SINGLET, TINGLES
M
N   NESTING, TENSING
O
P
Q
R   RESTING, STINGER
S   INGESTS, SIGNETS
T   SETTING, TESTING
U
V   VESTING
W STEWING, TWINGES,
      WESTING
X
Y
Z   ZESTING

	EHIRST		EILNST
A	HASTIER	A	NAILSET, ELASTIN, ENTAILS, SALIENT, SALTINE, TENAILS
B		B	
C	CITHERS, RICHEST	C	CLIENTS, STENCIL
D	DITHERS	D	DENTILS
E	HEISTER	E	TENSILE
F	SHIFTER	F	
G	SIGHTER	G	GLISTEN, SINGLET, TINGLES
H		H	
I		I	LINIEST
J		J	
K		K	LENTISK, TINKLES
L	SLITHER	L	LENTILS, LINTELS
M	HERMITS, MITHERS	M	
N	HINTERS	N	LINNETS
O	HERIOTS	O	ENTOILS
P	HIPSTER	P	PINTLES, PLENIST
Q		Q	
R		R	LINTERS
S		S	ENLISTS, LISTENS, SILENTS, TINSELS
T	HITTERS, TITHERS	T	
U	HIRSUTE	U	LUTEINS, UTENSIL
V	THRIVES	V	
W	SWITHER, WITHERS, WRITHES	W	WINTLES
X		X	
Y		Y	
Z	ZITHERS	Z	

EILRST

A REALIST, RETAILS, SALTIER,
   SALTIRE, SLATIER
B BLISTER, BRISTLE
C RELICTS
D
E LEISTER, STERILE
F FILTERS, LIFTERS, STIFLER,
   TRIFLES
G GLISTER, GRISTLE
H SLITHER
I SILTIER
J
K KILTERS, KIRTLES
L RILLETS, STILLER, TILLERS,
   TRELLIS
M MILTERS
N LINTERS
O LOITERS, TOILERS
P TRIPLES
Q
R
S
T LITTERS, SLITTER, TILTERS
U LUSTIER, RUTILES
V
W
X
Y
Z

EINRST

A NASTIER, RATINES, RETAINS,
   RETINAS, RETSINA, STAINER,
   STEARIN
B
C CISTERN, CRETINS
D TINDERS
E ENTIRES, ENTRIES, TRIENES
F SNIFTER
G RESTING, STINGER
H
I
J
K REKNITS, STINKER, TINKERS
L LINTERS
M MINSTER, MINTERS
N INTERNS, TINNERS
O NORITES, OESTRIN, ORIENTS,
   STONIER, TRIONES
P PTERINS
Q
R
S INSERTS, SINTERS
T STINTER, TINTERS
U TRIUNES, UNITERS
V INVERTS, STRIVEN
W TWINERS, WINTERS
X
Y
Z

145

EIORST

A
B
C   EROTICS
D   EDITORS, SORTIED, STEROID,
    STORIED, TRIODES
E
F   FORTIES
G   GOITERS, GOITRES, GORIEST
H   HERIOTS
I
J
K
L   LOITERS, TOILERS
M   EROTISM, MOISTER,
    MORTISE, TRISOME
N   NORITES, OESTRIN, ORIENTS,
    STONIER
O   SOOTIER
P   REPOSIT, RIPOSTE, ROPIEST
Q
R   RIOTERS, ROISTER
S   ROSIEST, SORITES, SORTIES,
    STORIES, TRIOSES
T
U
V
W
X
Y
Z

ELORST

A
B   BOLSTER, BOLTERS, LOBSTER,
C   COLTERS, CORSLET, COSTREL,
    LECTORS
D   OLDSTER
E   SOLERET
F   FLORETS, LOFTERS
G
H   HOLSTER, HOSTLER
I   LOITERS, TOILERS
J   JOLTERS
K
L   TOLLERS
M
N
O   LOOTERS, RETOOLS,
    TOOLERS
P   PETROLS
Q
R
S   OSTLERS, STEROLS
T   SETTLOR
U
V   REVOLTS
W   TROWELS
X
Y
Z

A	ATONERS, SENATOR, TREASON
B	SORBENT
C	CORNETS
D	RODENTS, SNORTED
E	
F	
G	
H	HORNETS, SHORTEN, THRONES
I	NORITES, OESTRIN, ORIENTS, STONIER
J	
K	
L	
M	MENTORS, MONSTER
N	
O	ENROOTS
P	POSTERN
Q	
R	SNORTER
S	STONERS, TENSORS
T	STENTOR
U	TENOURS, TONSURE
V	
W	
X	
Y	
Z	

A	NATURES, SAUNTER
B	BRUNETS, BUNTERS, BURNETS
C	ENCRUST
D	
E	NEUTERS, TENURES, TUREENS
F	
G	GURNETS
H	HUNTERS, SHUNTER
I	TRIUNES, UNITERS
J	
K	
L	RUNLETS
M	STERNUM
N	STUNNER
O	TENOURS, TONSURE
P	PUNSTER, PUNTERS
Q	
R	RETURNS, TURNERS
S	UNRESTS
T	ENTRUST, NUTTERS
U	
V	
W	
X	
Y	
Z	

EORSTU

A
B
C   COUTERS, SCOUTER
D   DETOURS, DOUREST,
     ROUSTED
E
F
G
H   SHOUTER, SOUTHER
I
J   JOUSTER
K
L
M   OESTRUM
N   TENOURS, TONSURE
O
P   PETROUS, POSTURE,
     POUTERS, SPOUTER,
     TROUPES
Q   QUESTOR, QUOTERS,
     ROQUETS, TORQUES
R   ROUSTER, ROUTERS,
     TOURERS
S   OESTRUS, OUSTERS,
     SOUREST, SOUTERS, TUSSORE
T   STOUTER, TOUTERS
U
V
W
X
Y
Z

GINOST

A   AGONIST, GITANOS
B
C   COSTING, GNOSTIC
D
E
F
G
H   HOSTING
I
J
K   STOKING
L
M   GNOMIST
N   STONING
O   SOOTING
P   POSTING, STOPING
Q
R   SORTING, STORING,
     TRIGONS
S   STINGOS, TOSSING
T
U   OUSTING, OUTINGS,
     OUTSING, TOUSING
V
W   STOWING
X
Y
Z

100 STRANGE WORDS

Frequently, a Scrabble® player will inform his opponent that his rack contains such awful letters that he cannot make any word at all. Often true, but often an exaggeration. This list is a haphazard section of 100 weird words from *The Official Scrabble® Players Dictionary*.

You may never get an opportunity to play any of these words, and even if you could play one it might not be your best move, anyway. Even so, to be aware that such outlandish-looking words do exist and could be used if necessary may be some consolation to you at some time. Even the most abysmal set of letters on your rack *might* contain some esoteric but allowable word.

ACNODE	ENZYM	KRIS	RHABDOM
ADUNC	EPHORI	KWACHA	RHYTA
APNOEA	EVZONE	LLANO	RYOT
ASPHYXY	FADO	MBIRA	SADHU
AUREI	FLUYT	MITZVAH	SANJAK
BDELLIUM	FORB	MOSHAV	SECCO
BLYPE	FRAKTUR	MRIDANGA	SFERICS
BONACI	GALYAC	MUZHIK	SOFTA
CEDI	GHARRI	NAEVI	SOVKHOZ
CHARQUI	GHERAO	NGWEE	SQUUSH
CIBOL	GHIBLI	NYLGHAI	SVARAJ
CIVIE	GOLEM	OGDOAD	SWARAJ
CRWTH	GUAIAC	PASQUIL	SYBO
CYANO	HAAF	PEYOTL	TAEL
DAWK	HAIKU	PIBROCH	TAUTOG
DHAK	IGLU	PSST	TMESIS
DJINNY	IKEBANA	PYKNIC	TOFU
DWINE	ISSEI	QIVIUT	TOPHI
DYAD	JEZAIL	RAGI	TOYO
EIGHTVO	KIVA	RATO	TREF
ELEVON	KLEPHT	REBEC	TSKTSKING

UNAI	VERA	VUGH	WYND
UNCI	VIREO	WATAP	YAMUN
URAEI	VOLTI	WILCO	YCLEPT
VANG	VROOM	WISHA	ZEMSTVO

5
VARIATIONS

Different games that can be played on a Scrabble® brand gameboard.

There are many variations that can be introduced into the game. House rules can be introduced, certain categories of words that are normally barred may be allowed, certain categories of words that are normally allowed may be barred, extra tiles can be incorporated into the game, time limits can be introduced, words can be totally dispensed with, and the game can be played in foreign languages. A number of the variations are examined here in more detail.

VARIATION NUMBER 1
Using the official rules, some players impose a limit on the number of times that a player may exchange his letters during the course of a game. Some players choose three, and some choose four. Some players do not allow a change of letters if there are seven or less tiles in the unused pool.

VARIATION NUMBER 2
The use of obsolete words may be barred, even though they may appear in the agreed dictionary. For example, the most widely used dictionary for Scrabble® in Great Britain is *Chambers Twentieth Century Dictionary*. This contains many obsolete words, and most players and clubs in Britain do not allow such words, even when they appear in Chambers.

VARIATION NUMBER 3

Some players impose a time limit for each move that players make. There may be a blanket limit of two minutes per move. Some players prefer to be more flexible, while still retaining the idea of a limit. They use chess clocks, where a player is allowed a total amount of time for all his moves, say, thirty minutes, but how he chooses to divide up this time between individual moves is up to him. If he needs only ten seconds to consider a certain move, all well and good. If he has a particularly tricky situation to ponder, he may well feel like using seven or eight minutes of his total allotted time. This is a good idea, the main problem being the accessibility of chess clocks.

VARIATION NUMBER 4

Some players introduce a very short time limit for each move, say, fifteen seconds. In such a "speeded-up" version of the game, there is very little time to think or plan ahead. It is very much a question of making the first reasonable score that you can see, and then not getting too upset when you realize that you missed a 50-point bonus. A quickie game like this can be used to fill in an odd fifteen minutes or so.

VARIATION NUMBER 5

The rule regarding the use of a dictionary solely to check a word's allowability when it has been challenged may be abandoned. There are two ways in which players are allowed to use the dictionary. In the first one, all players are allowed to make as much use of the dictionary as they wish at any time during the course of the game, looking for words to play. In this game, ideally, each player should have his own copy of the (same) dictionary. A different way of allowing players access to a dictionary is to allow its use only while their opponent is making his move. This method puts the pressure on player number two to complete his turn as quickly as possible. After all, the more quickly player two goes, the less chance there is of player number one finding a useful word in the dictionary. Allowing dictionaries to be used during the game, before words are played, is a good way to enlarge players' vocabularies, especially young players and novices.

VARIATION NUMBER 6

The official rules state that once a blank has been played, it cannot be moved. This particular variation, though, allows a player to pick up a blank from the board, replacing it with an equivalent tile. For example, if the word UN*ILED was on the board (with the * representing the letter T), then at a later stage, any player may take the blank and put down a real T in its place. A player is not allowed to put down a letter that is different from what the blank was originally stated to be, even if a new word results. If UN*ILED was on the board, a player is not allowed to pick up the blank, replace it with an F, and make the new word UNFILED, even though that is a word. There even are variations on this variation. One of them allows for such a substitution play to take place *instead* of a player putting letters on the board or exchanging letters; another version allows for a player to make such a substitution play and *then* play or exchange letters. Try both versions, but be sure that all players fully understand the precise rules.

VARIATION NUMBER 7

If you have access to two Scrabble® brand crossword game sets with the same size tiles, put all 200 tiles into one pool. Though there are 225 squares on the board, it is most unlikely that all 200 tiles can be played. Play continues until no player can make a move and all have used up the agreed number of exchanges. Again, make sure that all players understand how all the scores are adjusted at the end of the game.

VARIATION NUMBER 8

The official rules do not allow for the use of proper names, but you might care to try a game or two where these are allowed. You might just choose to allow any proper name shown in your dictionary. You may want to go even further, allowing any place-names that appear in a chosen atlas or gazetteer. As long as all the players know the rules, there is no limit as to what proper names can be allowed.

VARIATION NUMBER 9

How about playing thematic crossword games? All the words played have to have some common theme. For example, if the theme was motoring, words such as CAR, GEAR, CLUTCH, and PISTONS would be quite acceptable. There may be one or two problems, though, in deciding whether a particular word comes within the bounds of the theme or not. This is not such a serious variation, though it may be fun to play with children or after you have had a drink or two!

VARIATION NUMBER 10

Take a standard Scrabble® brand set and split the tiles into two heaps. Put the consonants in one heap, and the vowels in the other. Treat the Y's as vowels, and put one blank in each heap. You now have two pools. Then play the game normally, allowing players to take their letters from either or both pools as they wish. If a player makes a five-letter word and needs to pick up five new letters, how many he takes from each bag is up to him. He might choose five consonants and no vowels, four and one, three and two, and so on. Though a blank may have come from the vowel pool, it may be used as a vowel or a consonant. The same applies to the blank from the consonant pool.

VARIATION NUMBER 11

Scrabble® can be played through the mail. Expensive as the mail system is, there are flourishing postal Scrabble®

players clubs. Players make their moves and receive their letters via a referee, or "games-master." The games-master plays no other part in the game at all. Of course, players have unlimited use of the dictionary before making their moves. This can also be an excellent way to improve one's Scrabble® vocabulary.

VARIATION NUMBER 12

A player without a face-to-face opponent or any postal opponents, perhaps wanting to while away the odd half hour or so, can immerse himself in any of the several solitaire versions of the game. In one version, all the tiles are placed face down, well-shuffled, and the player selects seven tiles. He attempts to make a word in the normal way, and scores it. Then, he selects from the pool the number of letters necessary, bringing his rack up to its usual complement of seven letters. In this version, he can make openings for himself, just as he would if he was playing in a two-player game. In a second version of solitaire, the player attempts to get as high a score possible at every move. After each move, he puts his remaining letters back into the pool, mixes them thoroughly, and takes seven new letters. Though the concept of making openings still applies, the likelihood of 50-point bonuses falls off dramatically. Bonuses can now only be achieved if the player is lucky enough to pull seven letters out of the pool that just happen to make a word. In both these versions of solitaire, the player can compare his latest scores with scores from earlier games.

VARIATION NUMBER 13

Another variation consists of *removing* letters from the board of a completed Scrabble game. It is relatively quick and can be played by any number of players. The winner of the preceding normal game begins, and each player follows in turn. Each player removes at least one and not more than six letters from the board, according to the following rules: the tiles removed at each turn must be taken from one word still remaining on the board, though not necessarily from adjacent squares; after each player's turn, all tiles remaining on the board must form complete words that are properly interconnected with all the other words. The game ends when all the tiles have been removed from the board or when it is impossible to continue without breaking the rules. Scores can be kept in two ways. Method 1: The letter tiles may be counted at their face point values as they are removed from the board, and the player who scores the highest total number of points wins. Method 2: Tiles are counted at values modified by the premium squares from which they are taken. Double-letter-score and triple-letter-score premium squares apply to the letters that are removed from them; and double-word-score and triple-word-score premium squares apply to the total value of the letters removed at the time that the premium square is uncovered. The winner is the player with the highest total score at the end of the game.

VARIATION NUMBER 14

One of the strangest variations is this one, where the use of words has been dispensed with. Players concentrate on making high-scoring garbled letter sequences. Players take letters from the pool in the usual way, always having seven at a time on their racks. The tiles are placed on the board in order to give the highest scores possible. All sequences of letters, whether they are words or not, are valid. Scores are calculated in the usual way. The game becomes an exercise in using the premium squares and the high-value letters without being constricted by the need to form words as well! The 50-point bonus is done away with, otherwise players would continually put down seven letters, claiming a bonus at every turn. The concept of challenging disappears, too. Without words, there is nothing left to challenge. All the associated problems about choosing dictionaries, allowing some words in them, but barring others, disappear as well. This variation doesn't turn out to be quite so anarchic as it may sound.

VARIATION NUMBER 15

Scrabble® brand crossword game tournaments are not so much a variation in the way of actually playing the game as an excuse for getting together anything from ten to fifteen people at a time, all playing the game and competing against each other. Every player will get to play the same number of games, usually three or four. The winner of the tournament is the player with the highest total wins after all the games have been completed. Within equal wins, cumulative point spread decides ranking.

VARIATION NUMBER 16

The game can be played in foreign languages. Playing in languages other than English is more than just a question of playing with a standard English set and putting down foreign words. Foreign sets include different numbers of letters, different distributions, different point values for some of the tiles, and even different rules. Foreign-language Scrabble® sets are available usually from specialist games shops. Among languages that are currently available are French, German, Spanish, Italian, Hebrew, and Russian.

Gyles Brandreth

At thirty-five, Gyles Brandreth is one of Britain's most prolific and successful authors, having sold over eight million copies of his many books. A dozen of his children's titles have appeared in the United States and his other books published in America include *The Joy of Lex, More Joy of Lex, The Puzzle Mountain,* and *Great Theatrical Disasters.* Since 1981, his weekly "Alphabet Soup" column has been widely syndicated throughout the U.S. and Canada.

Born in 1948 and educated at Oxford University (where he was a Scholar at New College and, like several British Prime Ministers before him, President of the Oxford Union), Gyles Brandreth is also a journalist who has written for most of Britain's top newspapers and magazines, a broadcaster who has made over a thousand appearances on radio and TV, a theatrical producer with three London hits to his credit, the founder of the British championships with respect to the Scrabble® Brand Crossword Game, a former European Monopoly Champion, and the holder of the world record for the longest-ever after-dinner speech—twelve and a half hours!

He has lived in Hollywood, Baltimore, Washington, D.C., and New York, but now lives in London with his wife, who is also a writer, and their three children, who all have unique English names: Benet, Saethryd, and Aphra.

According to the *Scottish Sunday Post,* "Gyles Brandreth is the most likeable genius I've ever met!" According to the *London Daily Mail,* "Gyles Brandreth is the sort of person that a breakfast cereal company would would give their right arm for. He's bursting with vigour, fizzing with happiness, sizzling with vim and *Cosmopolitan* magazine once picked him as one of England's most eligible bachelors, though he was actually married at the time." According to the *London Sun,* "Gyles Brandreth is a writer, talker, wit and diversified character with a bowling-over effect on anyone he meets."